ENOUGH

OLIVIA JARAS

ENOUGH

A WOMAN'S JOURNEY TO
SELF-EMPOWERMENT
AND WEALTH

Published by Advantage Books, Charleston, South Carolina.
An imprint of Advantage Media.

ADVANTAGE is a registered trademark, and the Advantage colophon is a trademark of Advantage Media Group, Inc.

Printed in the United States of America.

10 9 8 7 6 5 4 3 2 1

ISBN: 978-1-64225-988-9 (Paperback)
ISBN: 978-1-64225-987-2 (eBook)

Library of Congress Control Number: 2024925210

This publication is designed to provide accurate and authoritative information in regard to the subject matter covered. It is sold with the understanding that the publisher is not engaged in rendering legal, accounting, or other professional services. If legal advice or other expert assistance is required, the services of a competent professional person should be sought.

Advantage Books is an imprint of Advantage Media Group. Advantage Media helps busy entrepreneurs, CEOs, and leaders write and publish a book to grow their business and become the authority in their field. Advantage authors comprise an exclusive community of industry professionals, idea-makers, and thought leaders. For more information go to **advantagemedia.com**.

*To the courageous women who dare believe in the idea
that we are and have always been enough,*

*those who dare venture beyond the safe harbors of conformity
and embrace the vast, uncharted ocean of possibilities.*

This book is a tribute to your unwavering spirit.

*May it serve as a compass, guiding you to unleash your boundless
potential, for great ships are not meant to remain idle, but to sail boldly
into the unknown, leaving trails of inspiration in their wake.*

CONTENTS

ACKNOWLEDGMENTS

I would like to express my deepest gratitude to the individuals who have played a significant role in the creation and completion of this book. Without their support, guidance, and unwavering belief in this project, its realization would not have been possible.

First and foremost, I want to thank my children, Maya and Lu. You have been my constant source of inspiration and motivation. Your presence in my life has ignited a fire within me to strive for a better legacy, not only for you but for everyone who aspires to break free from the limitations we impose on ourselves. Your belief in my abilities and your unconditional love have propelled me forward, even in moments of doubt. Your presence has been a pillar of strength, and I am grateful for the gift of being your mother.

A heartfelt thank-you to the women who have graciously shared their stories and experiences. Your courage and vulnerability have added depth and authenticity to the narrative, amplifying the voices of countless women around the world. It is through your willingness to be heard that we can inspire others and foster a community of empowered women supporting one another.

Finally, I want to express my gratitude to the readers of this book. Your curiosity, open-mindedness, and willingness to challenge limitations are a testament to your commitment to worthiness and empowerment.

And, of course, I'd be remiss if I didn't extend a big, heartfelt thank-you to those who doubted me along the way. Your impact has been immeasurable, and I am forever grateful for your presence in my life.

PROLOGUE

As I write this, I'm sitting at home. I've been crying for hours, waiting for the vet to come put down my best friend and darling girl, a golden retriever named Skipper. Skipper was diagnosed with a very aggressive type of canine lymphoma cancer about a month ago, and in spite of our best efforts, the cancer has spread everywhere throughout her body to the point that she's really struggling. She's suffering and is in a lot of pain. Last night was quite horrendous as I saw her restless, choking on her saliva, and gasping for air. Neither of us slept. We've tried everything we could, but that inevitable moment of death is coming.

I'm certain this is not quite the opening you expected for this book, nor the way I ever expected I would start it, but there's something so beautiful happening in this present moment, right as death is knocking on my sweet darling girl's door.

Skipper and I are doing what we always do best, snuggling on the couch while I read or write and try to make sense of the chaos swirling around me. She's happy in spite of the pain. It's quite honestly the perfect day. At least, I'm pretty sure Skipper feels that way. Though she's clearly swollen, uncomfortable, and loaded with pain medication, she's getting everything she's ever wanted. We've been joined at the hip since early last night, snuggling and cuddling on the couch, with me feeding her ice cubes and organic dried mango strips every couple of minutes. Plush way to go.

I'm capturing this moment forever on paper while my sweetheart Skipper is still here. In this moment, it's just us. And I'm taking it all in … the gift she's been to me and the gift we were to each other in this lifetime. I know I'll be hurting in a little while, but I also realize just how lucky I am to have loved the way I've loved you, my sweetheart.

Death is so scary. It has brought so much tragedy and grief to my life already. My grandparents, my father, my only brother, four miscarriages, friends, and, of course, other furry family members as well. It's never easy, nor does it get easier. And I'm bracing myself, because I know losing my girl in a few hours won't be easy … and once again I will be expected to bounce back and keep on going.

Keep going.

As women, we survive so many losses throughout our lives. Men probably go through the same thing, but I can only speak from my four decades of being a woman. We overcome more losses than any human should bear, and not only do we single-handedly internalize and mask our grief; we have this uncanny ability within us that allows us to ignore our pain and instead keep steamrolling ahead, showing up for everyone around us in whatever way they may need us. Everyone except ourselves. It's that juncture that we're going to journey through together in the pages ahead. That place where you show up for yourself and not for others, no matter what anyone thinks. That place where you're going to face yourself and let pieces of yourself go. That's the only way to truly understand your self-worth and place yourself firmly on the path to wealth.

And now Skipper is gone forever.

I held you tightly until your very last breath today. Just like I held you the day we first met. The day you came home to brighten my life and the life of everyone who met your loving gaze and irreplaceable smile.

How could I ever forget? We already had two dogs, and we weren't planning on a third one. But we went on our annual trek to the farm to pick up a side of beef to feed our family for the year, and you were there. It was instant. You and I recognized each other as soulmates on the spot, and there was never a doubt you'd be coming home with me. We were meant to be together, and that's how it was.

You were always by my side. And if I ever left home, you were the first one to greet me at the door, and you were the last one to wish me good night before the lights went out. You knew to cheer me up when I was down and to nudge me back to earth when I was getting lost in everyday anxieties. Without words but rather with your not-so-gentle nose nudging, with your loving eyes and smile, you always reminded me of the beauty of life that was happening around me. In your short five years on this planet, your unconditional love saved me from myself and my emotions more times than I could possibly count.

The void is real. The pain and loss are real. The screams inside my head cursing whoever is in charge of this nightmare are all too real as well. I can still feel your panting, and I can still feel your soft, warm fur. My hands still feel the gripping of you so tightly as you gave your last breath. As your heart stopped beating. Your puppy scent still lingers on me.

And the world in my head is pushing me to bottle it all up and keep going.

Keep going.

"Stop hurting, stop crying—life must go on. Everybody needs you to show up," says the stern voice in my head. I hear that voice trying to toughen me up and quiet the pain by telling me, "It was just a dog. Get over it."

But in my heart and soul, I know Skipper wasn't just a dog.

As women, we learn at a very young age that when we get hurt, we get back up, and we keep going. We don't give ourselves the chance to grieve, lick our wounds, and nurture ourselves back to health. Before we get a chance to shed our tears and feel the loss, we kick ourselves back onto our feet, soldiering away as we are supposed to do. Get back up, look pretty, be nice, and nurture the world around you.

We don't even notice that drop by drop, our cup becomes a little emptier each time we don't stop to acknowledge the pain, eventually leaving us in a void. Dry. Empty. We are left thirsting for something. A strange sense that a part of us is missing. Broken. Incomplete. Damaged. Unworthy.

And then we wonder why life isn't bringing us the joy and happiness we once believed we deserved. So we chase money, love, relationships, or "things" to quench our thirst. We try to love the rest of the world while our wounds are left to fester and bleed in the dark, where nobody can find them. We give from an empty cup, hoping one day we will feel that we are satisfied. That we are enough.

This book was meant to help you refill your cup and feel worthy of you, your dreams, and your right to claim your worth in this world. But right now it's just as much for me as it is for you. Because here's what I know: When I don't deal with that broken feeling, that sense of not being enough, the emptiness, the world reflects that pain right back at me in *every* area of life: love, joy, wealth, and satisfaction. It's one of those curiosities of life: If I gloss over my sorrows and keep moving forward, instead of treating myself as being worthy of healing my pain and nurturing myself back to wholeness, the world around me reflects that unworthiness right back at me. It glosses over me with pyrrhic victories, small wins that are unfulfilling and fraught with dissatisfaction because I never achieve enough.

So yeah, right now, I'm here struggling to feel unbroken and worthy. I'm feeling the pressure that it's not okay to nurture my wounds before moving on. But I know I need to do the work. The healing starts with me. Making the decision that I'm worth it.

I don't feel pride in saying to you that I've been down and back up this road way too many times. Maybe you, too, are here with me, holding a cup that needs filling. Or maybe you've been here for so long that you didn't even realize until now that you've been holding on to an empty cup.

Whatever brought you here, I'm sure glad that you and I can walk this path together. We're going to journey together, working out the kinks of your inner reality so that your outer world reflects the reality you and I both know it should reflect back to you. That happiness, that sense of satisfaction, and—dare I say it? Yes, wealth. That wealth that you deserve. May we raise our cups and promise each other that no matter what, we are in this together, until both our cups are full and we feel unbroken and worthy.

The truth is, I'm scared to write this book. I've written and rewritten this intro more times than my editors care to count. And in fact, I wrote this whole book and then decided to start all over again. Needless to say, my editors weren't thrilled. I've tried writing this book by doing a tech-free retreat at a remote-lake cabin in New Hampshire and in my surfer beach condo in Costa Rica, and I even spent a week locked down during a snowstorm in my art studio.

The weird thing is that it should be easy to write this book—after all, I am truly an expert at making money, negotiating money, and teaching women how to make more money. I can talk about tactics all day long, and that's what I did in the first version of this book.

But when I finished my first rodeo with this book, I felt a sinking pit in my stomach. The dire realization that something was missing. The same sinking feeling I get when I meet a woman who I *know* will not get paid what she really deserves. It's not because the tools aren't the exact ones you'll need, but I can't help you get from A to Z if nobody has taught you how to get to A in the first place. And if I'm honest, getting to A is the hardest part, because it requires you to make a very big decision. A through Z is a breeze—I'm willing to bet you've known your alphabet since you were a tiny little girl.

But the biggest decision you will ever make in your life is choosing to be worthy of making your own decisions or allowing the world around you to decide your reality for you.

This is a scary starting place for both of us. I'm asking you to make the biggest decision you will ever make, and in doing so, the message in this book requires me to open up to my biggest fear: that I'm not worthy of writing it and that it won't be good enough. But it's time to write this book, regardless of how uncomfortable my fears of rejection are making me feel, because even if all this book does is help you get you closer to your A, then I've done my job. Once you've glimpsed your true sense of worth and greatness, there's no going back. It'll only be a matter of time until you are equally complicit in changing the legacy for future generations of women to come.

Perhaps you are like me in that way as well. For too long, I cared too much about what others were going to think of me, feeling that I wasn't good enough, or the way I would be judged for what I did or did not do; after all, as a woman, I have spent over four decades desperately trying to get people to like me.

This book is about acknowledging that for women to go beyond financial equality, it has nothing to do with empowerment; rather, it's about vulnerability. Forging through that vulnerability is a journey that every woman who dares to build wealth beyond what is "expected" of her must take. That is the only way to call in the wealth and empowerment.

After having the privilege of helping thousands of women crack the code to pocketing millions of dollars they were leaving at the table, I know with absolute certainty that getting to wealth overflow is both technical and spiritual. But it's heavier on the spiritual than it is technical. The message I am meant to convey through this book is most certainly controversial and likely to be unpopular, at least in the beginning anyway (you'll see what I mean, and I hope you stay with me to keep delving further—I think you'll find it's worth it). I also know, deep inside my soul, that this book is meant to help usher in a new era for women and money. You might be thinking, *Who the heck does this woman think she is, thinking she's ushering in a "new" era?* More likely you feel completely turned off by the perceived arrogance of an author who thinks herself to be some divinely inspired messenger who is here to change the world. I get it—you've been conditioned to see people this way. And while maybe I won't get you to like me, I just need you to stick around long enough to start seeing things a little differently.

Because the truth is, you, too, are here to usher in this new era with me.

You see, we've all been told we're special while simultaneously being told that we are not—we are all equal. As women, we've been taught to hide our gifts from the world so that we don't rock the boat. If all I can do is put a tiny crack in this armor you've been wearing for so long, it will eventually get uncomfortable enough that you'll take it off for a moment and realize that you are being weighed down by it … and that you don't need it at all.

Personally, I have had the privilege of being cracked wide open by all the hurt and pain life has brought my way. And maybe you know what that feels like, and maybe, just like me, these lessons have brought you to your knees one too many times. Time and time again, we resiliently get up and get back in the game. We play by the rule book that has been handed down to us by generations upon generations. Yet as hard as you try, you can never seem to get ahead—the rules in the book just don't seem to make any sense. Always stuck living a life of struggle. Never happy, never satisfied, never financially ahead or feeling *fully* satisfied with our purpose in life. Eventually, though, women like us crack. We can't handle the struggle anymore, so we toss the rules out the window, only to realize that the rule book never applied to us anyway.

I'm here as someone who tossed that rule book out the window a long time ago, and I'm here to help you do the same. I'm here to aid and abet you into realizing you get to set the rules of the game of how life and success get to play out for you.

Society and rule-book followers will tell you I'm a bad influence on you, but I beg to differ. I'll be a really good influence on you. I'll be helping you get to where you want to go, both when it comes to purpose, self-worth, and, if it's your thing … wealth.

I've got your back. At the time of this writing, I've helped thousands of women crack open and increase our collective worth by tens of millions of dollars. *Their* worth, not their company's worth or their partner's worth. This is where you and I are going. I realize that sounds boastful, but I want you to know that I'm not saying this to impress you but rather to impress upon you that there's an underground movement of women like you and me who are choosing to unapologetically pursue that sense of knowing and embodying that we are *enough* ... and the inevitable consequence of shining the light back onto *you* is the financial freedom that comes pouring in.

We are going to deconstruct your sense of self-worth, take it apart, toss out what doesn't serve us, and rebuild using *only* the building blocks you choose. At times, you'll think I'm getting under your skin, but what I'm really doing is getting underneath that clunky, heavy armor you've been trained to believe defines you and your worth.

If you stay with me for the ride, not only will we have overhauled your own sense of self-worth, but just like every rebel woman before you who has ever tossed out the rule book, you will begin to feel an unequivocal sense of clarity, a strong sense of purpose and direction, and without even needing the steps from A through Z, you'll begin noticing you're making exponentially more money than you ever thought possible. As we venture on this journey together, remember this: you are a woman of immense worth. Both you and I know this already. When you believe in yourself and in your capability to shine, you bestow upon the rest of us the privilege of experiencing your gifts to this world. Let your unwavering determination guide you. Own your self-worth, ignite the fire within, and watch as the universe conspires in your favor.

Ready? Let's begin.

PART I

BUT ARE YOU REALLY ENOUGH?

We begin our journey by deconstructing what really holds most women back from earning what they deserve and what I've discovered is a true source of the problem—the unhealed wounds that we let fester until they shape our self-worth. We will then confront these deep wounds in our sense of self-worth, taking just a moment to acknowledge and nurture them but then breaking down the negative stories we've told ourselves for so long in order to begin rewriting the narrative. Of course, this journey wouldn't be complete if we didn't go digging deep inside to unearth those self-defeating scripts you've been holding on to for decades in order to begin recognizing that you are *enough*, that you can recalibrate your emotions and begin to see yourself as others do—not as a failure but rather as a resilient and accomplished woman who refuses to let life extinguish her dreams.

CHAPTER 1

THE RAGING TIDE OF INEQUALITY

Each time a woman stands up for herself, without knowing it possibly, without claiming it, she stands up for all women.
—MAYA ANGELOU

Have you ever found yourself grappling with the perplexing question of why, in the twenty-first century, we are still contending with a colossal gender money gap? Maybe this question has crossed your mind, or perhaps it's an issue that has never quite surfaced on your mental radar. But for me, it's been a persistent thought that has woven itself into the fabric of my existence.

Picture this: In the swinging 1960s and 1970s, women were earning a mere 60 percent of what their male counterparts got paid for the same job, sometimes even less.[1] Progress was slow, and it wasn't

---

1   Gloria Guzman and Melissa Kollar, "Income in the United States: 2022," US Census Bureau, Report Number P60-279, Table A-7, September 12, 2023, https://www. census.gov/data/tables/2023/demo/income-poverty/p60-279.html.

until the early 1990s that women clawed their way up to 70 percent.[2] Then, enter the COVID-19 pandemic, a wrecking ball that catapulted us back a century in terms of gender wage equality; the World Economic Forum forecasts that the gender pay gap won't vanish for at least 136 years.[3] That's over five generations of undervalued and underpaid women!

This quandary has occupied my thoughts for decades. I was diagnosed with ADHD at a very young age, but my parents chose not to tell me or do anything about it. Decades later when I found out about it (and was able to do something about it), I realized just how much I had missed out on growing up. I realize many people today believe ADHD is a myth, but I'm not one of them. The difference getting help made for me was like night and day. Growing up, I grappled with a pervasive sense of inadequacy. I felt stupid, dumb. I felt in my bones that everyone around me was smarter than I could ever be.

To make things worse, I had a persistent and dire thought always percolating in my thoughts: If intelligent and capable women were consistently falling behind men in their careers and compensation, what chance did I, with my shortcomings, have in the ruthless world of success? I was destined to fail.

I grew up in Santiago, Chile, raised in a society that instilled in me a tumultuous relationship with money—a sentiment echoed by women across all generations and geographies. We loved money when it graced our presence, loathed it when it vanished, and perpetually felt undeserving of it. Money became the barometer of our worth—only those with top grades were deemed worthy and, consequently, rewarded with financial prosperity.

---

2   Guzman and Kollar, "Income in the United States: 2022."

3   "Global Gender Gap Report 2021," World Economic Forum, March 2021, https://www3.weforum.org/docs/WEF_GGGR_2021.pdf.

Growing up in the 1990s, I've witnessed how the idea of money as a measure of worth became deeply entrenched in societal norms, especially for women. Even though my parents were big believers in gender equality, society subtly taught me that my value is closely linked to external markers of success, with financial wealth being paramount among them. These beliefs were reinforced by the cultural narrative that perpetuated the myth of the male "breadwinner" role. Unintentionally, and like billions of women across the globe, I found myself internalizing these norms, leading to feelings of inadequacy and unworthiness whenever I perceived myself as falling short in financial terms.

So when it came time to think about college, I made the bold decision to leave Chile, a move driven by a peculiar blend of societal expectations and a desire to escape my perceived unworthiness. Landing a spot at Tufts University in Boston felt like a lifeline, a chance to forge a new identity free from the constraints of those who knew me. Maybe I could run away and fool others into thinking I wasn't stupid.

Little did I know that my journey would lead me to a career in salary negotiations, human capital, and compensation, where I would assign and argue (in support of or against) the value of other human beings. While I've always loved this career path, I know I chose it as a desperate attempt to further hide my sense of unworthiness and fit into a world that seemed to measure my worth in dollars and cents. While my job allowed me to assess the worth of others, I could avoid measuring my "enoughness" at all costs.

Fast-forward to my twenties and thirties, when I found myself orchestrating salary decisions and negotiations for really big global companies. Though I was excelling at the career thing, I still clung to the feeling of unworthiness; in my gut, I knew I was less intelligent than my peers and that they would all soon find out that I was an imposter.

Then one day, I stumbled upon Sheryl Sandberg's article on the gender wage gap and the way companies were complicit in perpetuating it.[4] The article contradicted my belief that companies with compensation departments, like the ones I worked with, were champions of pay equality. I mean, my job was quite literally to ensure that people (regardless of gender or ethnicity) were being compensated fairly relative to market and internal equity.

Somewhat intrigued and disheartened by the article, I delved into my own data, setting out to prove that the gender wage gap did *not* exist. After all, I was the gatekeeper setting the salaries with great attention to any potential bias that could impact the pay ranges I was recommending to the hiring manager. And as the gatekeeper, not only was I female; I was also a minority.

I was confident that I would be able to refute this notion. But to my dismay, I proved to myself and my peers that, indeed, there was a significant pay gap between men and women. But for a different reason than Sheryl had pointed out.

In looking at thousands of salary recommendations my peers and I had given over the years, the evidence was clear: in spite of companies wanting to do "what's right," women were often settling for lower salaries due to a pervasive sense of unworthiness. They either didn't know their worth, or even if they did, they didn't know or feel worthy of advocating for it. This propensity to not advocate for ourselves can be caused by any number of factors, some of which are outside our control.

---

4   Sheryl Sandberg, "Sheryl Sandberg: Pay Gap Holds Us All Back," *USA Today* (op-ed), April 4, 2017, https://www.usatoday.com/story/opinion/2017/04/04/ pay-gap-women-equal-sheryl-sandberg-column/99954086/.

We've all faced moments of feeling inadequate, unworthy, and out of place. It's an acknowledgment of the challenges we've overcome and a reminder that in our darkest moments we have the potential to transform, much like an oyster forging a pearl amid years of irritation.

It's imperative that we do so if we're going to bridge the gender money gap. In fact, studies correlate self-worth to income and even suggest that it's a two-way street—self-esteem may increase income, and increased income (such as a pay raise) may increase self-esteem.[5]

My experience, and my opinion, is that the gender money gap isn't just a contemporary issue; it's a manifestation of generations of unhealed wounds, a legacy that continues to shape our perceptions of self-worth. To break this cycle, we must confront the deeper wounds within ourselves and across generations. It's not about vilifying the system but about recognizing our role in perpetuating the narrative of unworthiness and not *enoughness.*

This book aims to empower you to transcend the gender money gap, not through negotiation tactics (I've written other books to help with that) but by addressing the roots of underearning—our wounded sense of self-worth. The path toward earning what both you and I know you deeply desire to be earning begins with a process of healing, an acknowledgment and transformation of the lingering pain within. It begins by voyaging through your vulnerabilities and reconnecting with that baseline assurance that you are enough. Without this

---

5   Francesco Drago, "Self-Esteem and Earnings," IZA Discussion Paper No. 3577, IZA Institute of Labor Economics, July 14, 2008, https://papers.ssrn.com/sol3/papers.cfm?abstract_id=1158974; Charlotta Magnusson and Magnus Nermo, "From Childhood to Young Adulthood: The Importance of Self-Esteem during Childhood for Occupational Achievements among Young Men and Women," *Journal of Youth Studies* 21, no. 10 (2018): 1392-1410, http://doi.org/10.1080/13676261.2018.1468876; Lex Borghans, Angela Lee Duckworth, James J. Heckman, and Bas ter Weel, "The Economics and Psychology of Personality Traits," *The Journal of Human Resources* XLIII (2008), 4, https://jenni.uchicago.edu/papers/Borghans_Duckworth_etal_2008_JHR_v43_n4.pdf.

fundamental understanding, any success will prove fleeting and lack permanence. This is a journey, a clear invitation to move beyond restrictive stories about yourself and actively shape your path to a happier, more satisfied, and wealthier you.

Here's to you, boldly embracing your absolute brilliance and recognizing that you are unequivocally enough, shattering the glass ceiling, and rewriting the narrative for yourself and for future generations of women. Here's to a world where every woman not only acknowledges her true inner worth but stands tall and unapologetic with bank accounts brimming with dollars and assets in her name.

CHAPTER 2

TELL ME HOW YOU REALLY FEEL

Nothing has a stronger influence on children than the unrealized and unlived dreams and lives of their parents.
—CARL JUNG

In our lives, there comes a point where we recognize the weight of money-related baggage that isn't truly ours—fears, stories, and baggage accumulated over the years. Acknowledging this burden becomes crucial, and though we may convince ourselves that mere awareness will suffice for healing, we fail to see the direct correlation between this baggage and our financial reality. Consequently, we find ourselves wondering why we still can't command the income we deserve or make our business flourish. I like to think of it this way: realizing that you are carrying a rucksack full of rocks is *not* the same as putting the rucksack full of rocks down.

The struggle arises because these beliefs, like all thoughts and emotions, reside in the intangible realm of our minds, making it challenging to pinpoint and confront them definitively. We acknowledge that we are unnecessarily carrying heavy rocks, but we don't do anything about it. We might settle and pretend that money isn't the primary focus, telling ourselves, "It isn't all about the money anyway ..." But is it not? Kind of like pretending those rocks aren't weighing you down.

Let's check in with your amygdala for a moment. Does it protest, telling you that money is evil, that only bad people have wealth? Do you vilify people who have private jets, fancy cars, or mega yachts? Does it question the importance you give to pursuing wealth for your own happiness? If so, let it voice those concerns, and I'll be here, patiently waiting with my coffee (or tequila), knowing you'll return.

Now, shall we continue?

While it's true that money doesn't equate to intrinsic worth—you were born worthy, a miraculous outcome of the chance. I mean, what were the odds of that sperm meeting that egg, on that planet that happens to be among billions of other planets that don't support life as we know it, with a sun at the exact right distance to not burn us into smithereens?

I don't know about you, but those realizations about existence always give me cause for celebration. Yet our "highly" sophisticated human society has chosen to use money as an external measure of a person's worth. We live in a world where success is gauged by dollars and purchasing power, a reality we may dispute but are conditioned to accept.

In today's social media–driven world, the relentless pursuit of perfection amplifies the belief that material wealth defines our worth. Though these platforms may serve the purpose of keeping us connected to friends and family, they also fuel the comparison culture, perpetuating the notion that success is measured in likes and followers, further deepening feelings of inadequacy.

Our feelings about money, whether happy, sad, or stressed, are reflections of something within us. Our emotional response to money, be it joy, sorrow, or anxiety, serves as a mirror reflecting our innermost beliefs. And while we may continuously assert that our inherent worth is not tethered to wealth, the stark reality is that societal norms dictate otherwise. We've unconsciously agreed to narratives, passed down through generations, that shape our worldview and align us with societal expectations. Our inherited stories lead us to perceive the world as our community does. This means that our sense of "enoughness" often becomes entwined with societal standards, particularly those revolving around financial success.

Here's the harsh truth, though: we are conditioned to do this. Looking at it from an evolutionary standpoint, accessibility to resources has always been crucial for species survival. Throughout human history, our ancestors learned to prioritize the acquisition of resources like food, shelter, and protection to ensure their survival and the continuation of their lineage. This instinctual drive for resource accumulation has become deeply ingrained in our psyche over millennia, influencing our perceptions of success and worth in modern society.

Today, money is the medium for accessing those resources. The more money you have, the more comfortable your survival is. Money has become a survival mechanism ingrained into our modern society.

If my statement above makes you feel kind of "yuck," not only does that prove my point that you are still carrying heavy rocks on your back; it creates the contrast relative to the warm fuzzy feeling I want you to have about money and wealth. Acknowledging the problem is always the first step, putting down the rocks is step two, and finally, deciding what to carry in your rucksack (if you even want to carry it in the first place!) happens when you and I rewire your narrative going forward.

Here's where tuning in to yourself unleashes a narrative that's undeniably empowering for women. Survival in today's world reveals a powerful advantage for women. You see, accumulating wealth isn't just about survival of the fittest anymore. In this new arena, women possess a distinct competitive edge. Despite past conditioning that may have caused many women to doubt their worth, we now have the opportunity to thrive in a domain where our strengths are not only equal to but often surpass those of our male counterparts. In fact, in 2019, young women earned at least as much as their male counterparts in 22 of 250 cities in the United States.[6]

So yes, you have a competitive advantage over men when it comes to making money.

You just haven't tapped into it … yet.

Let's get one thing straight: this book isn't about pointing fingers at men for the wage gap or about pointing fingers at women for falling short. We point enough fingers at ourselves as it is. It's about doing something altogether different with your hands. Stop pointing altogether, and start turning the genius that is you into wealth. Your gift can translate into myriad revenue streams if you choose to allow it to. I urge you to set aside notions of inequality or even equality. The truth is, men and women were always destined to be different, and by homing in on your distinct qualities and your genius zone, you gain a competitive edge that secures your success regardless of your gender. It also sets the stage for a brighter future for generations to follow,

---

6   Richard Fry, "Young Women Are Out-Earning Young Men in Several US Cities," Pew Research Center, March 28, 2022, https://www.pewresearch.org/short-reads/2022/03/28/young-women-are-out-earning-young-men-in-several-u-s-cities/.

generations that will learn from you to stay busy making magic with their hands rather than pointing fingers at each other.

In this new playing field, the market will happily pay your commanding rate as long as you can back it up with absolute certainty of your worthiness. Money is a renewable resource, generated through production, trade, and investment. Unlike natural resources, money can be consistently generated, recycled, and redistributed.

Don't believe me? Consider this. Our system that was once limited to bartering pelts and rocks and subsequently backed by gold has evolved into a global network of wealth circulation. In 1959, the total amount of currency in circulation in the United States was approximately $33 billion. Fast-forward to today, and that figure has skyrocketed to over $2 trillion.[7] This exponential growth showcases the renewable nature of money, constantly expanding in spite of inflation, debt, cost of living.

And as we journey deeper into the emotional complexities surrounding money in the chapters ahead, remember this: I'm not asking you to flaunt your money; rather, I want you to feel inherently deserving of financial abundance. It's okay if you're not fully buying into my words yet, but journey along with me, and I promise your financial reality will change drastically. You might not be ready to put down those rocks you are carrying, but over the next few chapters it's bound to get mighty uncomfortable. You'll feel less and less inclined to vilify your boss, rich celebrities, and YouTube billionaires.

So once your amygdala settles again, activating your prefrontal cortex—that part of your brain that affects your personality, behavior, and ability to self-regulate and plan—we'll embark on the transformative process of shedding the emotional baggage that's kept your sense

---

7 "Currency in Circulation: 1917-08-01 to 2024-05-01," Federal Reserve Bank of St. Louis (FRED), accessed June 21, 2024, https://fred.stlouisfed.org/series/CURRCIR.

of being *enough* confined under a glass ceiling. Grab your journal and pen, because the journey toward financial liberation and self-worth begins now.

I'll guide you through journaling prompts, often sharing not only my own writings but also entries from real women who've undertaken this transformative work before you. Why journal? Because when you write, you release, tapping into answers already within you but often drowned out by the day-to-day noise. Let it all out, and you'll come to find that writing is a very effective way of putting down those rocks you've been carrying.

It is my absolute certainty that if you let the pen wield more power than you, it becomes a direct line to those untapped answers residing within.

So, for your first exercise, open up a journal (it doesn't have to be a fresh one, but it should have plenty of open pages, because we are really going to be putting that thing to use with this book), and then pen down this declaration:

"The pen knows more than I do."

Next, let's set an intention for what you aim to achieve—a goal. Don't fixate on the look and details of the outcome but rather on how *you* get to feel once you arrive at that goal. It doesn't need to be perfect or final, but every journey requires a destination. Where are we headed? (Yes, I'm coming along for the ride.)

Here are some example intentions:

- Kate: "I feel burdened by the baggage we all carry as women, especially since the COVID-19 pandemic. My intention is to declutter the mindset of trash talk holding me back. I want to feel that I belong, that I am doing enough. That I *am* enough."

- Sarah: "I want to move past this block; I feel like I'm constantly moving but never reaching my destination. I want to feel that I have enough. I want to feel good about myself or what I've accomplished; I want to expect more wealth than I have thus far and not feel ashamed of it."

- Audrey: "I aim to overcome the fear and anxiety that paralyze me, hindering my accountability for career growth. I want to be friends with money, not fear it. I want money to work for me, not me work for money."

- Akaylah: "I intend to change the beliefs I've inherited, particularly the scarcity mindset from my parents' troubled relationship with money."

- Rebecca: "Working long hours for too little—something needs to change. My intention is to have more money and work less and not feel guilty. I want to feel good about making loads of money and not being a slave to working endless hours."

- Kerry: "My goal is basic but crucial. I lack focus in everything, including my new business. I want to feel focused with my vision, because I know that will inevitably bring in loads of money."

Do any of these resonate with you? In my years guiding women through this exercise, every intention, without exception, connects to something perceived as lacking or unworthiness. The truth is, you already possess the solutions; you just need to tap into them.

> Now let's set your intention:
>
> "My intention is to ..."

Let's continue our journey. Our goal is to identify the tip of the iceberg that's been holding you back from earning what you truly deserve. To get you to earn more, we need you to feel worthy of more. In order to get there, we must uninstall the old software and throw the rule book out the window. Put the rocks down.

Fair warning: my prompts are designed to get this junk out of your system hard and fast. You'll be ripping off the Band-Aid, and it'll hurt. There will be plenty of tears and moments you'll likely be muttering to yourself, "Oh f*ck, this is too painful."

There will be times when you'll feel like ditching this book or setting me aside. "We" can take as long as you need on this journey—I'll be here, ready and waiting for you.

But when you do set "us" aside, I want you to remember this: your external reality is a direct reflection of your internal reality. When you find yourself again at the end of the month with not enough to pay your bills or afford the life you want, you'll know you haven't cleared the junk, and I'll be right here waiting for you to continue on this journey.

So why not make the commitment to unleash your full potential? Right here, right now is your moment to courageously tackle the challenges you've been avoiding. Seize this present opportunity to not only transform your financial future but also to shape the financial legacy for generations of women to come. Let everything within you flow freely. Approach it with determination, and witness how your rucksack begins to get lighter while your bank account and sense of self-worth flourish exponentially from the outset.

I'm right here beside you on this transformative journey. The aim of this book is to carve out a nurturing space for you to delve into the depths of the iceberg that may be hindering your sense of worth (rucksacks, icebergs—you're probably beginning to realize I love visual analogies. Plenty more coming your way!). While there's undoubtedly more beneath the surface, our initial focus is on gaining awareness of the iceberg's core. Together, let's begin unraveling its layers and empowering you to navigate toward greater self-discovery and fulfillment.

Let's take a look at what lies underneath the surface, shall we? Grab your pen and notebook, and complete the following prompt:

"At my [insert your current age] years of age, I have the feeling that my life resembles [...] more than it resembles the life of a [...]."

Let your reaction be immediate, and write your response as visceral and as detailed as possible. This allows you to see your conditioned response, shaped by decades of letting your mind run wild. Your mind has likely already formulated a response, and it will likely let you know all the ways in which you've failed at life. I want you to write it down—let it flow. I'll be right here, popcorn and tissues in hand.

Need inspiration? Here's my example when I first did this exercise:

"So at thirty years of age, I have the feeling that my life resembles a carnival of missed opportunities, served with a main dish of failure and repressed potential for dessert. I am an absolute abject failure of a human being more than it resembles the life of a successful woman who has been given every opportunity in life."

It was scary to let that out, but it felt like such a relief. Because once it was out there, it was no longer festering inside me. I put that big boulder down and chose to never carry it again.

Need even more inspiration? Here are examples from other women in my workshops:

- "At my fifty-two years of age, I have the feeling that my life resembles a pile of shit. A lot of failures, hatred, self-doubt, a lot of 'why me?' constantly, like being tense and like being taken advantage of."

- "At my forty-six years of age, I have a feeling that my life resembles someone who is an emotional cripple, unable to move forward in my interpersonal and public or career life, unwilling to risk making progress, more than it resembles the life of anyone worth admiring, someone who would be considered successful in any part of her life, a creative genius, unapologetic in her success."

- "At my thirty-seven years of age, I have the feeling that my life resembles disorganized chaos, where I feel like a failure to others and to myself and a misfit in society, looking for shiny objects as answers/solutions."

- "At my twenty-eight years of age, I have the feeling that my life resembles my mom's, my scarcity beliefs, my traumas, and trying not to make mistakes, more than it resembles being able to speak up, having a mutual, loving relationship, being free and not afraid of making mistakes, having that full potential and abundance in the relationship."

Notice the trend? We tend to believe we should have been someone else, should have been living a different reality by now. Isn't that batshit crazy? It's *wild* how for most (all?) of us, our primary sentiment of who we are just leads us to this place of not only automatically assuming but *declaring* the worst of ourselves? That we're faulty, that we're intrinsically bad and sucking at life?

The most impactful part of this exercise is recognizing that we've carried these feelings for so many years. This journal entry reveals the tip of the iceberg that keeps you earning less than you deserve, settling for mediocre opportunities, and stifling your potential to thrive. Isn't it astonishing to think that you've allowed yourself to feel this way for so long?

This is exactly what I mean when I say we need to get to A before we can go from A to Z. Do you see that what we're currently experiencing is just the surface of a much larger issue that prevents us from even getting started on this journey? No wonder we end up taking subpar opportunities, earning less than we deserve, and restricting the development of our full potential.

Personally, the most mind-blowing part of this reflection is realizing that most of us grapple with these feelings of unworthiness for decades—or even lifetimes! So let's talk about how we start to move beyond this and step into our own power.

CHAPTER 3

LET'S DIAL DOWN THE CRITIC, SHALL WE?

You've been criticizing yourself for years, and it hasn't worked.
Try approving of yourself and see what happens.
—LOUISE HAY

S o now we've had a glimpse of how you truly feel about yourself. And let's be real—if you breezed through that exercise above, spewing only rainbows and unicorns about yourself, then congratulations! You're a master of disguise, but let's face it—you're probably faking it in a lot of other areas of life too. I dare you to go back and unleash the real deal.

Armed with what we've learned through those first exercises, let's delve deeper into the transformative step you've just undertaken. Having confronted your genuine feelings about yourself, the next step is to recalibrate those emotions. Frequently, we tend to perceive our reality in a more negative light than it actually deserves. The objective here is not to ignore the ugly or dismiss our challenges but rather to acknowledge the positive aspects that coexist with the difficulties.

To achieve this shift in perspective, we're going to need to shower ourselves with some serious self-love. But considering the emotional roller coaster you just described, asking you to suddenly start writing love letters to yourself might be a bit much, don't you think? So here's the deal: the next prompt is all about breaking free from that relentless negativity and embracing a more balanced, empathetic, and dare I say uplifting view of your life's journey. But let's face it—expecting the same ol' version of you to suddenly switch gears is like asking a cat to bark—it's just not going to happen. So let's shake things up and invite a fresh perspective to the party, shall we?

For this one, step out of your shoes and imagine stepping into the shoes of an unbiased observer, detached from self-judgment. What narrative would this impartial observer craft about your life's journey?

Here's what I wrote when stepping into my unbiased observer shoes:

Damn, she's gone through a lot. She's had a lot of ups and downs in her life. So much death, so much loss. And yet she is still here. She's so strong. Crazy to think she is still standing. She's so resilient. I don't think many people would have survived, let alone thrive, through what she's gone through!

Here's what Susan's unbiased observer wrote:

She's so hard on herself. She's not even forgiving herself. She's forgiven everyone else except herself; she's so ashamed of what she's done, though she should be so proud. She's accomplished so much. Look at that résumé—she's done a lot. She's done all of it. The grit and resilience she had to develop in order to endure. Every time she fell, she got up stronger.

Here's what Emma wrote:

I understand why it happened the way it happened. She was conditioned by other people intentionally or unintentionally. So she told herself she could do better. She didn't have good examples around her, so she became the example. I'm so proud of her.

Now it's your turn.

Take five to ten minutes to spend some time with your unbiased pen (which, I'll remind you, knows more than you do!), and write down what an observer might say about you and your life.

Isn't it interesting how we can go from being so cruel to ourselves to being so kind?

When reading the initial responses from other women, I notice a common trend of being excessively critical and brutally unforgiving toward ourselves. However, there's an equally powerful turning point where recognition of accomplishments and the development of grit and resilience emerge. It involves embracing the understanding that external influences, whether intentional or unintentional, have played a role in shaping our narratives.

We think that kind version of us doesn't come from within us, but the truth is, that impartial observer is still *you*.

The shared sentiment across these impartial reflections is the profound sense of empowerment and relief that accompanies the shift in perspective. It's your own recognition that, despite enduring substantial challenges, there's a wealth of strength and accomplishment to be acknowledged.

The act of acknowledging the impact of conditioning, or in Emma's case understanding the absence of positive examples and becoming her own example, is a powerful shift in perspective. Sure, acknowledging the pride in your journey underscores the importance of self-compassion and acceptance, but more importantly, it sheds light on that proud version of you that, while perhaps dormant, *still* lives within you.

You see, by the conclusion of this book, we will have unearthed your vulnerabilities in order to truly root that highest empowered, wiser, and most aligned version of you. The version of you that knows how to call in wealth by relying on herself and herself alone. Stay committed to this journey alongside me, and watch as that mighty, self-assured queen reclaims her throne. Those pesky, negative narratives swirling in your mind will be subdued and placed back in their rightful confines.

By the way, there's one more thing I'd like to share about the journaling prompts I'll be asking you to complete as we move through this journey. While the choice is yours on how deeply you engage in these entries, consider this: Breezing through a chapter or skimping your way through these exercises could cost you more than you realize. Refusing to acknowledge your worth means settling for less, sabotaging opportunities, and perpetuating self-limiting patterns. Deciding to take the time for yourself to deal with all the baggage you are carrying is a gateway to transcending limits, seizing opportunities, and cultivating empowering new patterns. Envision this as an act of self-empowerment, crafting a future where your potential flourishes, confidence soars, and financial success becomes an achievable reality.

Plunge in with fearless enthusiasm, and I promise you'll witness transformative results. These prompts are your stepping stones to a brighter, more fulfilling narrative. Right here is your opportunity to redefine your story and unlock the incredible possibilities that await you. The transformations are yours to claim.

In short, the work we are doing is a transformative process that will challenge you and your negative self-perceptions. I guarantee that, at multiple junctures, your inner critic will try to persuade you to stop. It'll try to convince you that those heavy rocks are there for a reason. Perhaps try to tell you they are a defense mechanism that came in handy once and may come in handy again soon.

Just keep showing up for yourself. We need to unearth these festering beliefs in order to rebuild a foundation of self-worth. This shift in mindset is fundamental to your feeling worthy enough of pursuing opportunities and earning what you truly deserve. It's your turn to break free.

All right, now that we've checked out the tip of the iceberg, are you ready to cannonball in and see what really lies underneath? Time to dive off the deep end!

CHAPTER 4

TRACING LITTLE DEATHS

Healing is not about forgetting; it's about remembering differently.
—UNKNOWN

Fair warning—when I meant diving off the deep end, I really meant it. We're tackling the tough stuff head on. I know you're not here to just tread water—you want to see real, tangible change, and you want it now. Well, you're in luck, because I have faith in your resilience. You've got a wealth of memories, some carefully tucked away, others purposefully buried. And deep down, you know that confronting those dark, locked-up memories is key to unlocking the life you've dreamed of.

So let's cut to the chase. How about we dust off those memories you've been avoiding? You know the ones—the ones you've tried to push to the back of your mind, to ignore, to breeze past, to forget because they hurt too much. It's time to face them head on.

In my home country of Chile, there's an expansive highway called the Panamericana. It intricately weaves through the very soul of the nation, linking Patagonia's enchanting icescapes all the way to the expanses of one of the driest places on the planet. Every summer, my parents would pack up the car, and we'd embark on a seven-hour journey north on the Panamericana from Santiago to Morrillos, a desolate beach nestled where the desert meets the Pacific Ocean. Despite its remote location, Morrillos teemed with life during the summers. Morrillos wasn't just a destination for me—it was a sanctuary where countless summer memories were forged.

But I digress. Along the journey from Santiago to Morrillos on the Panamericana, as the landscape unfolded from greenery to dry vastness, I would count the *descansos* along the road—small, solemn memorials at the roadside, each one marking a life tragically cut short, prompting me to reflect and wonder how each one of those lives was cut short, how many dreams were left unfulfilled, and how their families were handling the grieving.

What does this have to do with buried memories? Consider those markers along the Panamericana as a lens through which we view our lives—a collection of "small" deaths and losses, experiences that altered the very fabric of our existence.

Our lives are adorned with these descansos, those pivotal moments that demanded an abrupt change in direction, a recalibration, often without the luxury of proper mourning of the loss we experienced in the process. Perhaps we were too young, or responsibilities weighed too heavily on us, to stop and give ourselves the love and care we deserved. The grieving never happened, and while we may have blocked the memory, our soul hasn't forgotten.

My descansos tell a poignant tale, marked by profound moments of loss and transition. From leaving my homeland of Chile to embrace a new life in the United States to grappling with the untimely passing of my father and beloved only brother, each chapter etches its own sorrowful imprint. The heartache of enduring four miscarriages, the anxiety of my husband's deployment to Iraq, deaths of loved ones along the way—all are moments of loss that further shaped the landscape of my journey. And yes, the loss of my faithful companion Skipper is most certainly another descanso on my journey.

Yet, amid these descansos, we often find ourselves hurtling forward, caught up in life's relentless pace, overlooking the vital necessity of grieving our losses. Those pivotal moments, etched into the fabric of our existence, deserve more than a passing acknowledgment. Without the intentional embrace of grief, these wounds linger beneath the surface, quietly accumulating emotional weight. And in the haste of pressing on, we inadvertently carry the burden of unhealed pain, and as time elapses, these unresolved emotions resurface, limiting our potential and impeding our journey.

This is precisely why you and I will dedicate the necessary time to mourn and acknowledge the profound impact of these descansos. Far from a display of weakness, looking at how deep your sorrows run is a courageous act. All these moments of true pain and loss have caused little twists and turns throughout your path, defining your course just like the weather and environment can define how a tree grows. But they don't get to define who you are. You can be a crooked tree, but that doesn't prevent you from flowering and blooming delicious fruit. Looking at our descansos allows us to understand the twists and bends on our path with the empathy of someone with the understanding of hindsight.

So let's cast our gaze backward and take stock of all those descansos in your life that deserve acknowledgment and grieving. I find the best way to do this exercise is to get creative and draw. Of course, if you prefer to write them out, please do so.

If you're going all Picasso with me on this, begin with a starting point on one corner of the sheet, and from it, draw a road that begins on the day you took your first breath, winding its way to this very moment. Begin placing little crosses along this road, each marking a descanso, a moment that forever shifted the course of your life, and inscribe the name of the "little death" on each cross. While these inscriptions might seem meaningless to others, mere blips on the radar, you and I both know they were seismic shifts that altered the very landscape of your life. It doesn't matter how insignificant it may seem; if it was a meaningful loss to *you*, it deserves a cross, and it deserves a name.

Now, consider this: Between each of these descansos, we often find ourselves in a perpetual forward motion. Life's demands, societal expectations, and our own ambitions compel us to keep moving, sometimes without pausing to nurture and heal the wounds inflicted by these moments of profound change. It's as if we're on a continuous journey, the road stretching endlessly, and in our eagerness to move forward, we inadvertently neglect the crucial pit stops needed for self-care and introspection.

These descansos, scattered along the highway of our lives, often become mere milestones as we speed past them, brushing off the need to reflect on what they really meant for us. The reality is, each one deserves more than a fleeting acknowledgment—they warrant a moment of stillness, a pause to honor the pain, the consequences, the growth, and the seismic shift they triggered within us. It's not just about marking the descansos on the map but allowing ourselves the time to release the agony and pent-up emotions we tried to ignore.

Why are we doing this? Because you and I both know that turning a blind eye to those seismic experiences that forever altered your life doesn't make them disappear; it only gives them room to fester in the darkness. Today, you're bravely exposing them to the light, transforming these sore spots into intricately woven threads within the beautiful tapestry that is your life.

To give you another example, consider these descansos from my Ukrainian friend, Iana, who wrote these down during one of our workshops and found herself giving voice to grief that she had not realized she was carrying so heavily:

+ The brutal loss of my best friend at age ten and the childhood emotion I held for thirty years

+ Aggression from my father

+ Not making the volleyball team in high school

+ Separation from husband

+ The death of my father

+ That one big fight with my mom, and how I never apologized

+ Being fired from my job

+ Escaping the war in Ukraine

Once you're done with your drawing, I want you to close your eyes for a moment. Acknowledge these descansos; let the weight of their significance wash over you. Instead of rushing past them, as per our usual automatic pilot, I want you to pause here for a moment to truly grasp the sheer magnitude of everything you've endured. Yet despite their relentless onslaught, you've emerged as a testament to the power of the human spirit, surpassing the bounds of what seems humanly possible to endure.

That little girl within you, who weathered storms and put on a brave face, deserves more than just passing acknowledgment. She deserves a standing ovation for the masterful performance she put on when the world demanded strength and resilience. Now, let's honor your strength—the very essence of what we now call you—that emerged from those moments, because they have laid the foundation for the extraordinary woman you are today.

After you complete your map of descansos, take your pen and write a letter to your younger self, acknowledging those descansos. Pour your heart into each one, expressing deep admiration for the strength you had to summon in order to carry yourself through every time.

Here's what Iana wrote:

> I'm so sorry, my dearest young self. I never stopped to realize just how hard we've had it. It was never easy, was it? I can't believe you made it through all of this and more with a smile. It's amazing that we made it through everything and that we are still here.
>
> I'm so proud of you and how we've turned out. We are so strong. So beautiful. I wouldn't be here today if it weren't for you. Those were tough lessons with death. And you didn't deserve the treatment from your father, Nobody deserves

that. But you've learned, and your daughter will live a better life because of it.

While you couldn't see why things happened the way they did back then, know that it all happened for a reason and that it all turns out quite beautifully. Your bravery, determination, and resilience got us through it all. I can lovingly and clearly see that I owe it all to you.

I love you so much, my dear young self.

Iana

Keep this letter close to your heart. You'll be grateful to have it nearby when tough times inevitably resurface. For as much as this letter speaks to the you of the past, it also serves as a guiding beacon for the future you, reminding you of the resilience you possess to overcome whatever challenges lie ahead.

Like my friend Iana, though your life may look much different from hers, we often brush off each of those moments without recognizing their weight and the pain they inflicted. It's a burden no one should have to bear, navigating through such challenging experiences. Yet here you stand, a testament to your resilience and bravery in facing them head on. I applaud you for the courage it took to acknowledge and map out those descansos, marking each one with honesty and vulnerability along the way.

CHAPTER 5

BURNING AT BOTH ENDS OF THE STICK

The light within us is a flame that can never be extinguished by the darkness that surrounds us.

—UNKNOWN

I find fairy tales resonate deeply with me because they tap into fundamental aspects of the human experience, offering profound wisdom, comfort, and inspiration.

In the heart-wrenching tale "The Little Match Girl," penned by Hans Christian Andersen in 1845, we are transported to the chilling streets of Copenhagen during the bitter winter months, amid the festive holiday season. Here, a fragile orphaned girl navigates the unforgiving streets, her tattered rags failing to shield her from the biting cold. Barefoot and alone, she carries the heavy burden of selling matches, her small figure fading into the wintry landscape as the bustling crowds pass her by, their indifference casting her into shadow.

As she shivers in the chill, the matches become her companions, each one possessing the potential to kindle a brief spark or light a roaring fire. But in her youth and ignorance, she knows not how to nurture a roaring fire. So with each light of a match, we catch glimpses of her dreams and aspirations, a glimpse that quickly fades back into darkness. Each strike is a plea for warmth, not just for her freezing body but for the yearnings of her innocent heart.

The girl lights the first match to warm herself, and in its glow, she sees a vision of a warm stove and a sumptuous feast. This image feels so real, it almost provides her with temporary relief from the cold and hunger.

As the match fades, she quickly strikes the second match and envisions a beautiful Christmas tree adorned with lights and decorations, evoking a moment of warmth filled with joyous celebrations, reminding her of the warmth and love she longs for.

Each subsequent match illuminates a fleeting moment of happiness and comfort for the little match girl, offering brief respite from her harsh reality before quickly fading away.

Not wanting to let go of those beautiful moments, she strikes one match after another. As she continues, a solitary star twinkles in the night sky. Its gentle glow envelops her, evoking a sense of comfort and warmth. For in that starry sky, she had heard that departed souls find solace, watching over those they've left behind.

As that match fades, she is fast to strike another one from her dwindling pile, bringing on a vision of her deceased grandmother who embraces her lovingly and makes her feel warm, loved, and finally at ease.

As the tender vision of her grandmother begins to fade away, the girl, overcome with desperation and longing, frantically strikes another match. And another. And another. Tears blur her vision as she ignites each match, desperately clinging to the fleeting moments of solace and connection. In one last bittersweet moment, the girl begins to rise into the skies, held in her grandmother's arms.

The next morning, the girl's lifeless body is discovered in the snow.

To me, the profound tragedy lies not only in the little match girl's physical coldness and death but in her innocent lack of understanding about the need for kindling and nurturing a fire. Her matches, though a source of transient warmth, flicker out quickly, mirroring the ephemeral nature of her attempts to find solace. She didn't know those matches could make a roaring fire. This is such a powerful reflection of how often we, like the little match girl, don't realize the necessity of cultivating and nurturing our aspirations, dreams, and potential. In our relentless pursuit of wealth and success, we light many matches—initiate endeavors—without recognizing the importance of kindling and sustaining the flame. This oversight can leave us in the chilling cold of missed opportunities and unfulfilled potential.

I like to think of the little match girl's tale as a metaphorical mirror, urging us to not only strike matches but to conscientiously kindle and nurture our flames, as we will need them to blaze brightly against the hardships we inevitably encounter in life.

Furthermore, in the pursuit of the temporary flicker of a match, we often overlook the fuel locked within our past because we fear that our past failures will define or hurt us. Yet these perceived failures are not anchors but rather kindling waiting to be ignited, lighting our path to success and illuminating the strength and resilience within us to achieve unimaginable heights.

Now, think of your own life. When have you been a little match girl? When have you lit matches and chased a flicker of light to your own detriment? I'm certain that if you try, you can recall at least five matches you've ignited, only to find you didn't know how to nurture the flame. You tried to spark something, but the fire never took hold.

Perhaps you were too naive or were so hooked on the shiny object that you neglected to nurture the flame. Regardless of the reason, the flame fizzled out.

Perhaps a time when love consumed you, a blazing inferno of passion within your chest? An emotion so intense, it felt like it was meant to be. Yet, despite pouring your heart into it, the love you offered wasn't reciprocated, or at least not reciprocated the way it should have been. It wasn't your fault; there was simply no kindling to nurture the fire. And when the flame finally extinguished, it left behind a searing emptiness and that all-too-familiar ache of unrequited love and heartbreak.

Or the time when you had that brilliant business idea. The one you dived into with unwavering dedication, determined to make your vision a reality, certain it would change the future for you and generations to come. Yet, despite your relentless efforts, you lost steam. External challenges and unforeseen hurdles emerged, smothering the flames before they took hold. It wasn't a lack of commitment on your part; it was the absence of the kindling of adaptability and resilience in the face of adversity. As the brilliant idea fizzled out, you were left grappling with the bitter taste of failure and unworthiness.

Each of these moments are matches we've lit, each carrying potential brilliance. Yet the absence of vital kindling often leaves us out in the cold, underscoring the need to cultivate elements for sustained success and fulfillment.

Here's the key: we are not bringing these up to blame or excuse the extinguishing of these flames but rather to acknowledge them so that the voids left by these instances no longer haunt and limit your potential and future.

Doesn't it break your heart to witness many women, upon reaching a certain point in life, convince themselves they've exhausted their matches? They toss in the towel, opting to freeze in place rather than chase the flame—the very essence of who they are. It's like their life is frozen in time, their ambitions extinguished.

But I know for a fact that if you find yourself reading this book, you are just like me in that you refuse to let life trample over your big, scary, ambitious dreams. We are destined to live expansive, joyful, and fulfilled lives at whatever cost. Even if it requires taking inventory of our matches—both ignited and waiting—and discern the kindling we already have or need to acquire in order to fan the flames of our dreams. And you know what's pretty incredible? All those matches you've burned over the years have amassed into a big mountain of coal, poised and ready to fuel the flames of your boldest dreams and aspirations.

> Time to grab a pen and paper again. You can write this out, or if you are more visual like me, draw it out like a tapestry or map of sorts. Organize it however you see fit, but the goal is to give you a clear vision of the lessons you've learned from those burnt matches so that you can forever remember how to nurture future matches into a roaring fire.

Here's what you will need to map this out:

- All your burnt matches (at least five of them)
- Your new understandings on what the kindling was that was missing for those matches to turn into flames
- How you can nurture your current and future dreams better with these new understandings

- A flame that's already roaring and one you want to start in the near future

I like to think of every match, whether ignited or not, as viable as coal, kindling, or a spark for a future ablaze with your brilliance. Reject the notion that you've run out of chances or that you failed when that match fizzled out; instead, embrace the fire of your inner power, using past failures as potent kindling. Your journey is extraordinary, and your future is waiting to burn with the flames of your badassery. Let the resilience within you kindle a new, brighter, more ardent flame.

PART II

TEARING DOWN

Now that you've discovered—and confronted—the source of the wounds to your self-worth and begun to recognize that the gender money gap stems, largely, from self-worth, it's time to begin rebuilding. That starts by recognizing and taking off the mask and then focusing on strengths rather than shortcomings. We'll start to reframe how you've approached and overcome challenges and then outline how to recognize and rid yourself of those who would rather let you sink than buoy you up.

PART II

CHAPTER 6

THE MASQUERADE

Life is a process of becoming, a combination of states we have to go through. Where people fail is that they wish to elect a state and remain in it. This is a kind of death.

—ANAÏS NIN

Imagine a pristine parking lot or a flawlessly paved surface, its smoothness interrupted by a lone crack. From that crack emerges a cluster of dandelions, defiant and unapologetic. Now, consider your initial instinct—most people feel an urge to uproot those dandelions, to restore order and conformity. Dandelions, in this context, are not celebrated for their beauty; they're dismissed as weeds, deemed "not appropriate."

Extend this metaphor to human interactions. When a woman appears where she is not expected or behaves in an unbecoming fashion, society often uproots her, forcing her back to where she supposedly belongs—with the other "weeds." This tendency is deeply ingrained in human nature. The more one stands out, the more discomfort, suspicion, or envy arises. It's a subtle erosion, chipping away at uniqueness until, almost imperceptibly, one gives in and conforms to the ordinary.

To me, the dandelion reflects the unfortunate reality that societal norms often stifle individuality, pressuring us to conform and blend in. It highlights the subtle yet pervasive forces that compel us to suppress our uniqueness in the face of societal expectations.

Imagine for a moment the enchanting resilience of a field of dandelions, each one standing tall and unique. These vibrant golden flowers are like women embracing their natural beauty, growing strong and proud in their individuality. Be the damn dandelion—even as the world blinds itself to the profound beauty found in uniqueness.

Society, much like a passerby dismissing dandelions as mere weeds, often fails to appreciate the strength and authenticity of women. Toddlers, much like these dandelions, start their journey believing in the power of their individuality. A child's cry for food or even their instinct to reach for a toy reflects an innate understanding of their worthiness.

As we grow, external influences subtly shape us. The messages that crying in public is discouraged or that we need a filter to be socially acceptable begin to erode our natural self-worth. Our concept of money is also shaped externally—by our family, our surroundings, the people we encounter over time. We're nudged to conform to a predetermined notion of appropriateness, of worthiness, disregarding the unique beauty that makes each woman a metaphorical dandelion in a world quick to label her as a weed. Despite these societal misconceptions, the essence of our authenticity remains as powerful and resilient as a field of dandelions in the face of disregard.

Over time, these messages coalesce into a sort of "mask" that we can put on in certain situations. We learn to behave in ways that are not authentic in order to either fit in or not be rejected by our tribe.

Over the years, our unfiltered, happy-go-lucky child is covered with these masks of who we should be and who we need to be in order to be accepted and/or valued by others. And eventually we begin to subconsciously believe that the masked version of ourselves is better and buy into the idea that the unfiltered version of us is just not good enough. Our lives become a veritable masquerade.

In wearing these masks to conform and please the world around us, we inadvertently hinder our ability to reach our full potential and attain success in life. The energy spent on maintaining these disguises detracts from the authentic power within, much like diverting sunlight from the growth of a vibrant flower. And all that energy, slowly seeping away, degrades our view of our self-worth—our perceived value in the world.

By shedding the layers of conformity, we not only reveal our vulnerabilities but simultaneously unleash the untapped potential that has long been obscured. Embracing our true nature is always scary because we expose ourselves to being judged or rejected. But just like a dandelion, you can only blossom when exposed to the light. Unmasking is the key to unlocking a wealth of possibilities and achieving financial success on our own terms.

As we start to realize that we have to cover up who we really are to either not be rejected by society or to fit into society, we began to accumulate these different masks, because without them, we're not accepted by the pack and or we're judged by the pack.

Whether it was chasing a trend, doing everyone else's homework, or overcommitting yourself to everyone else's interests, you started buying into a persona that allowed you to fit in. You see, at one point or another, we were all judged as not worthy of fitting in because we were just being who we are.

The majority of us had parents and other trusted adults who tried to help us overcome/heal our pain rather than change our understanding that we were never flawed to begin with. Instead, the message we got was to hide who we really were. Even if we were told by our loved ones to ignore the negative feedback, we heard the messages that the rest of the world told us. Rarely does society tell us, "Continue being you. Continue trusting your inner guidance system. Keep being your amazing, perfect self."

Instead, the message we internalize is "Let's change this and this and this about you, and let's figure out how to get you to conform. Excelling at conformity will make you happy." So we begin the process of becoming someone we are not.

We forgot that at our core we always were, and always have been, a masterpiece. We learned to cover it up, because somewhere along the line, someone who didn't feel worthy told you that you weren't worthy either.

In my case, the challenge was navigating an environment where I wasn't perceived as smart due to my attention-deficit problems. I had a really hard time focusing during class, and my grades reflected it. So I had to adapt to survive in one of the most academically rigorous schools in South America, an institution I often liken to a real-life Hogwarts. The setting was stringent, with formalities like a grand dining hall where headmasters presided from a raised platform, overseeing uniformed students partaking in silent prayers before lunch. Weekly assemblies and uniform inspections were the norm, with high academic expectations shaping the atmosphere.

Given the challenges of my unfocused mind, I crafted a persona— the girl who befriended everyone. Not hailed for academic prowess but valued as a loyal and dependable friend. This strategic move allowed me to lean on the academically gifted peers for homework assistance, clarifications on class materials, or support during challenging group projects. It became my protective mask, a coping mechanism shielding me from rejection within the academic herd.

It was so hard for me to read books and focus on academics that my only way to calm my anxiety was by watching others. I couldn't concentrate on books, but I could observe people for hours. I'd wonder what made them so much smarter than me. I would do this in class all day, every day. Either watching the cool or smart kids, or doodling on my notebooks, thinking about how or why everyone was so much smarter than I could ever aspire to be.

I didn't realize this at the time, but watching people was allowing me to decipher the things they weren't actually saying. It was almost like a heightened sense of intuition. Hours melted away as I observed, a silent spectator deciphering unspoken narratives. I read not only words but actions, vibes, and energies. I could tell when they were being honest or deceitful and when they lacked confidence or were just being defensive.

In a society where slenderness reigns supreme, my physique always leaned toward the curvier side, and in this landscape of rigid beauty standards, I felt the sting of rejection for not fitting the mold of conventional skinniness and beauty. Recognizing that this departure from the norm meant exclusion from the sought-after circles of popularity, I forged a coping mechanism. Becoming the congenial hostess of grand gatherings, I extended invitations to all, including the cool kids. My strategy was clear—forge connections, host grand parties, and let the allure of camaraderie bridge the gap that societal norms had imposed.

When it came to authority figures, I orchestrated a parallel game. While cracking the books eluded me, mastering the art of forging connections became my academic forte. On most days, during lunchtime, I sensed a tinge of loneliness in the demeanor of the headmaster, Mr.

Cowan, a grandfatherly figure, when no guests accompanied him. Seizing the opportunity, I ascended the high-rise to where he dined, extending a friendly query: "Mind if I join you for lunch?"

And like clockwork, he'd respond, "Miss Jaras, of course. I'd enjoy your company."

This mask kept me out of a lot of trouble, as all masks are supposed to. I'm a little embarrassed to admit this, but one time, a girl two years younger than me was hitting on my crush. He would eventually become my boyfriend, but at the time I had no love for her, so I brought a rotten yogurt to school, opened it, and put it in her backpack when nobody was looking. Then I stepped on it. (Yes, I know. Total bully move ... and I did regret it. Years later, I apologized to her.)

Everyone knew I'd done it, so I got called in to talk to Mr. Cowan. He stared at me and said, "Was this really you? It really surprises me that you would do something so unbecoming."

I looked him straight in the eye and said, "Of course not! If I was going to play a prank like that, I would have done something way more dramatic. Don't you think she probably just forgot she had yogurt in her backpack? I bet she's blaming me because she's jealous that we both have the same crush, and I suspect he favors me."

And I got away with it, because I had become so skilled at knowing exactly what needed to be said in response to reading the situation.

This skill of reading and persuading others to like me came at a cost, though. I began to buy into the idea that who I really was as a person was actually stupid. That I couldn't do anything unless I manipulated people into liking me. That's the problem with masks—they have benefits and drawbacks. In this instance, it kept me out of trouble, but it also took away my integrity. I wasn't being myself. I was being the girl I thought I was supposed to be because I feared the real me wouldn't be accepted. The truth is, you always give up a part of the real you when you put on a mask. And as I later realized, it not only hindered my personal growth but also limited my potential to earn more money and achieve greater success in the future, because a mask eventually makes you feel like a fraud, and that inevitably undermines your self-esteem.[8]

In our workshops, we always delve into the myriad masks we often don without realizing their profound impact. Consider the story of Becky, who identified as a high-achieving "all-rounder" from a young age. This mask served as her armor against bullying and the chaos of feeling out of control. Yet the cost of this security was significant. Here's a glimpse into our conversation during the workshop and Becky's journey of self-discovery:

Becky: I've always played the all-rounder. It was expected of me as the eldest child—to excel in everything from sports to public speaking. But it was more than just expectations; it was a survival strategy to prevent bullying and control my surroundings.

Olivia: Unmasking these roles is never easy, but recognizing them is the first step toward change.

Becky: The truth is, maintaining this mask has cost me relationships and personal fulfillment. I'm ambitious, yet I fear choosing myself or a partner because I might be seen as unstable.

---

8   Robin A. Berkley, Roxanne Beard, and Catherine S. Daus, "The Emotional Context of Disclosing a Concealable Stigmatized Identity: A Conceptual Model," *Human Resource Management Review* 29, no. 3 (2019): 428–445, https://www.sciencedirect.com/science/article/abs/pii/S1053482218300305.

Olivia: It's profound, but it's a crucial realization. Understanding the real cost of our masks—loneliness, missed opportunities, and suppressed true self—can liberate us.

Becky: I've been living up to a persona that made me lonely and limited my career. I saw myself as a leader, but it meant being alone. I now realize I don't want to live behind this mask anymore.

Olivia: Thank you for sharing. It's powerful to acknowledge these masks and their impacts.

Like Becky, many of us trade our true selves for acceptance, not realizing the full extent of what we lose—authenticity, dreams, potential happiness, the wealth we deserve, and so much valuable time. The introspective process of recognizing and shedding these masks is especially crucial for women because it has a direct impact on their ability to build wealth and achieve personal growth. The societal pressure to conform, to measure up to external standards, often breeds anxiety and self-doubt, hindering both personal fulfillment and financial success.

Reflecting on my personal experiences and those of many women I've had the privilege of working with, the fear of being "too much" or doing "too much" is a common source of anxiety. These pressures can feel overwhelming, but by tapping into our core, we recognize that our dreams and aspirations serve a meaningful purpose. I truly believe, though, that something greater than us, call it universe or a divine force, has imbued us with these visions for a reason.

By breaking free from the constraints of societal expectations and choosing to base decisions on what brings us happiness and joy, we empower ourselves to live authentically. Embracing a full day of varied activities without reservations, despite societal scrutiny, is a testament to living true to oneself.

Aligning with our true selves and exuding an unshakeable sense of worth allows us to transform into beacons of authenticity. This radiant authenticity not only captivates those around us but also inspires profound change. When women fully embrace their vulnerabilities, they transcend the ordinary, becoming influential masterpieces that inspire and empower others. And guess what inevitably follows? You awaken an unshakeable sense of self-worth that makes you an absolute money magnet.

Think about it: money always gravitates to strong, confident minds and scurries away very quickly from unworthy, anxious ones.

But let's get back to our masquerade, shall we?

I want to further explore and challenge the masks you wear. Pick that pen back up and work through this reflective exercise:

1. Draw a simple representation of each mask you wear in your daily life. Use any medium that feels right—pencil, paint, digital tools—and don't worry about artistic skill.

2. Next to each drawing, write a brief description of the mask's purpose. Why do you wear it? What does it protect you from, and what does it cost you?

3. Reflect on what your life might look like without these masks. Which ones might you be ready to shed?

This exercise is not about judgment; it's about awareness and choice. It's an opportunity to understand the roles you've assumed and to decide if they align with the person you truly want to be. Embrace this exploration of your authentic self, untainted by external expectations. Consider the liberation and empowerment that come with being your true self, and inspire others by illuminating the path toward authenticity.

CHAPTER 7

SAMURAI CREED

I am the master of my fate; I am the captain of my soul.
—WILLIAM ERNEST HENLEY

When my first child entered the world, overcoming postpartum depression and shedding the pregnancy weight became a strenuous, year-long battle. Then, just two weeks after celebrating Maya's first birthday, I found myself in the shower, feeling an all-too-familiar wave of nausea. It hit me like a jolt—this wasn't part of our five-year plan. As I dried off, my mind raced to the weight I had worked so hard to lose, now potentially on the brink of a rebound.

Predictably, the pregnancy test confirmed my suspicions. Excitement mingled with apprehension. The realization of undergoing another pregnancy journey, from the nine-month wait to nursing a newborn, overwhelmed me. I questioned my ability to endure it all again.

As I always did in times of distress, I immediately called my older brother (and best friend) Benji, who was studying Mandarin in China at the time, to share the news. Although my anxiety was palpable, he knew exactly what to say to provide me with the unwavering support only a best friend can deliver in such moments.

Then came my selfish admission: "Dork!" (Yes, that was my affectionate nickname for him.) "I have no idea how I'm going to handle this. I can't bear to gain the fifty pounds I did last time."

His response was a game changer. "Don't stress about it. It'll unfold as it's meant to. You're bringing another family member into our lives; let's focus on that. But once this kiddo arrives, you and I are training for that Half Ironman triathlon in Pucon (southern Chile). We're going to crush it. You'll be in the fittest shape of your life."

In that moment, he talked me off the ledge, soothing my worries and leaving me with a newfound determination. "Don't worry. We've got this. I'm going to train with you. We're doing it together." His assurance and commitment became the catalyst for turning trepidation into anticipation, setting the stage for an unexpected but empowering journey ahead.

As I hung up, a sense of assurance settled within me that everything would somehow be okay.

A mere week later, a very unexpected call from my brother's girlfriend interrupted me in the middle of my workday. Her voice, usually absent from my phone, echoed with urgency and fear. Excusing myself from a meeting, I hastily answered, already feeling the weight of unease.

Before I could fully step out of the room, her trembling voice delivered the shock that would alter everything. "Please tell me this has happened before!"

"Calm down," I urged, struggling to comprehend. "I don't know what's happening. What's going on?"

The desperate narrative unfolded—my brother clutching his chest, collapsing, unresponsive. Panic gripped her. "I can't get him to breathe. I have no idea who to call. Your mom isn't answering. Please tell me what to do!"

I assured her that nothing like this had ever occurred before, instructing her to call an ambulance. The urgency in her voice heightened. "I don't speak Mandarin!"

Guiding her through mouth-to-mouth resuscitation, I urged another friend in the room with her to raise the alarm and yell down the hallway. "This is an emergency. Someone will understand your distress."

The ambulance arrived forty agonizing minutes later, long after Benji was gone.

The word *heartbreaking* couldn't encapsulate the pain. The loss of my brother and best friend shattered me in a way no previous grief had. Despite having weathered the loss of grandparents and my father and enduring four miscarriages, this was unparalleled. Benji, unequivocally the person in my life closest to me, was gone. A cherished relationship with its secret language, daily conversations, now silenced. I would miss him indefinitely, and I even more intensely began to feel the pressing nature—and value—of time.

My subsequent pregnancy was an arduous journey—emotionally, physically, and psychologically. Consumed by grief, I indulged in excess, and as I entered the delivery room, I carried more than seventy pounds of additional weight.

Postpartum depression came back in full force with the birth of my second child. But so did another pivotal moment of choice: either let the pain define my outlook, or declare, "F*ck it. You're not going to drown me." You can call it divine intervention. Call it massive stubbornness and determination. Whatever it was, I decided that I was going to do the impossible.

I was going to go for that triathlon Benji and I were supposed to do together in Pucon. And the universe opened up avenues for me. I connected with Benji's college bestie and training partner, Carlitos.

He coached me and became my training champion the way Benji would have been.

I trained for over a year to get ready for the triathlon race in Pucon, and it took all my heart and soul to show up through all this without Benji. While the physical training was demanding, the emotional journey was even more arduous.

After congratulating me at the finish line of the race in Pucon, Carlitos told me that they had just announced that the US National Half Ironman Championship was happening in Miami that year, literally in Benji's old neighborhood. Then he said, "You'd be an idiot to not see this as a sign."

Of course I saw it as a sign!

Now, I'm a fit, muscular girl. I'm not cut out to be the kind of cyclist or runner who climbs hills. But Miami is as flat as a pancake. I can do flats.

Aside from the fact that it was being held in Benji's city, everything around this race was aligning for me in incredibly mysterious ways.

So I, of course, showed up on race day and completed the race that Benji had challenged me to do. In the end, I took fifth place in my age group, which landed me a spot on Team USA.

Team USA!

Through life, we are often presented with seemingly insurmountable obstacles. Soul-crushing experiences that truly make you either sink or swim. I could have sunk under the sorrow and the loss. I could have let my physical self go. It would have been easy to say my newly gained seventy pounds of extra weight were too many to deal with and just stop looking in the mirror. But something kept me going, reminding me that I was better than that.

That "something" that sparked within me is in everyone on earth. It is the seed of the masterpiece we can be, not the disaster we often think we are. And when we tap into that seed, we can do anything—we can be our fullest self; we can succeed at what we set our sights to. This applies just as much to athletic endeavors as it does to financial ones.

> *The women whom I love and admire for their strength and grace did not get that way because shit worked out. They got that way because shit went wrong, and they handled it. They handled it in a thousand different ways on a thousand different days, but they handled it. Those women are my superheroes.*
> **—ELIZABETH GILBERT**

I had support through my trials, and for that I am beyond grateful. But in the end, it was me who had to get out of bed and put on those running shoes every day. It was me who had to get out of my sorrows and show up for raising my kids, being a wife, and going to work. It was me who had to pursue my athletic dreams despite the dozens of extra pounds that were oozing out of every item of clothing I owned. Ultimately, we have to decide within ourselves that we don't have to rely on the stories of others or on other people to get us through. We can use our thoughts to our advantage or as a weapon to destroy ourselves.

To harness our inner strength and confront life's grand ambitions and challenges, we might take inspiration from the discipline and philosophy of the samurai. Samurai warriors dedicate their lives not only to mastering their martial skills but also to cultivating a profound sense of honor, worthiness, and identity. Central to their way of life is a powerful creed, dating back to the 1300s, that instills a frame of mind focused on self-reliance and inner strength.

Each morning, the samurai dresses facing the sunrise, fastening twenty-one ties on their samurai-style robe. For each tie they fasten, they recite one of the twenty-one creeds of strength and virtue they have memorized and adapted to make their own.

Can you imagine just how powerful it is to start your day by asserting (from memory) your twenty-one strengths and virtues? Most of us wander through life not knowing if we have any virtues at all, let alone listing them.

So you can probably guess what you and I will be doing next. We're writing out your own adaptation of your twenty-one creeds. You don't have to go by the book on this one, but I do want you to write twenty-one strengths and virtues that make you proud when you recite them in the mirror every morning.

A lot has been lost in language translation and over the centuries, but below is approximately how the Samurai Creed reads:

1. "I have no parents; I make the heaven and earth my parents."

2. "I have no home; I make awareness my dwelling."

3. "I have no life and death; I make the tides of breathing my life and death."

4. "I have no divine power; I make honesty my divine power."

5. "I have no means; I make understanding my means."

6. "I have no magic secrets; I make character my magic secret."

7. "I have no body; I make endurance my body."

8. "I have no eyes; I make the flash of lightning my eyes."

9. "I have no ears; I make sensibility my ears."

10. "I have no limbs; I make promptness my limbs."

11. "I have no strategy; I make 'unshadowed by thought' my strategy."

12. "I have no designs; I make 'seizing opportunity by the forelock' my design."

13. "I have no miracles; I make right action my miracle."

14. "I have no principles; I make adaptability to all circumstances my principles."

15. "I have no tactics; I make emptiness and fullness my tactics."

16. "I have no talents; I make readiness my talent."

17. "I have no friends; I make my mind my friend."

18. "I have no enemy; I make carelessness my enemy."

19. "I have no armor; I make benevolence and righteousness my armor."

20. "I have no castle; I make immovable mind my castle."

21. "I have no sword; I make absence of self my sword."

I am, of course, not suggesting you appropriate samurai culture, especially if it is not one you have any heritage of within yourself, but there is value in considering the meaning behind these ancient practices and the effect it had on those who performed them. There is immense value in starting each day by focusing on our strengths rather than our shortcomings. Can you imagine the transformative impact of applying a similar practice tailored to affirm your own worth and capabilities?

It's time to get that pen back out and create your own daily affirmations.

1. Reflect on your life's journey, and list twenty-one

values and strengths that make you proud. Each should resonate deeply and reflect a personal victory or a cherished aspect of your character.

2. Write yours as the Samurai Creed above, or alternatively, write them as affirmations:

   - "I am [your name], who overcame [challenge]."

   - "I am [your name], proud of [achievement]."

   - "I am [your name], a champion of [personal value or trait]."

- For example:

   - "I am Olivia, a proud mother of two amazing kids."

   - "I am Olivia, a woman who stands for my own self-worth and the worth of others."

   - "I am Olivia, the woman who qualified for Team USA."

3. Once you have your list, place it where you will see it *every morning*—on your mirror, next to your coffee machine, or on your car's dashboard. Make it a ritual to recite these affirmations as you start your day, reminding yourself of your worth, your strengths, and your accomplishments.

This practice is not about boasting; it's about reinforcing the reality of who you are and the steps you've taken to arrive where you are. By affirming your worth daily, you empower yourself to tackle ambitious goals and embrace your potential for wealth and success. Embrace this ritual, and watch as it transforms your mindset, your day, and eventually your life.

Then, just like the samurai, your daily ritual will help you master your sense of worth. It will begin to abolish any doubts about the true value that you bring and empower you to believe in your worthiness in all areas of your life, including wealth. It will help you evolve your mindset to a positive one, one where you deeply understand—and take charge of—your relationship with money.

As your sense of self-worth grows, you'll feel the load of your rucksack begin to lighten and the masterpiece behind your vulnerabilities begin to emerge.

See where we are going here?

CHAPTER 8

TOASTING YOUR TRIUMPHS AND UNVEILING THE UNDERDOG

I n this pivotal chapter of our journey, we're going to transition from peeling back the layers of self-doubt to cultivating a potent, unwavering money mindset. This transformation begins with a celebration of your resilience—the cornerstone of your newfound sense of worthiness. As we toast to your past triumphs, we lay the groundwork for future financial empowerment.

So get that pen back out, open your journal to a fresh page, and let's revisit five types of triumph that have shaped your indomitable spirit:

1.   The Unseen Challenges You Overcame

Take a few minutes to journal about the times you conquered obstacles that no one else even knew existed. Maybe you completed a project at work under tremendously tight deadlines while managing personal turmoil no one was aware of. Maybe you were able to budget for a special gift or trip that you never thought you could afford, or you paid off a debt, such as a mortgage, earlier than expected. This isn't just about professional success; it's about recognizing your ability to juggle multiple battles, invisible to others but monumental to you.

2. The Times You Outshone Doubt

Can you remember a time when everyone doubted your capabilities? Perhaps it was a public speaking engagement or leading a major project for the first time. But despite the naysayers, you didn't just perform; you excelled, showcasing your leadership and poise under pressure. This was not a stroke of luck but a testament to your preparation and resolve. Write about that moment, and what it felt like, for five to ten minutes.

3. The Creative Solutions You Engineered

Think back to a moment when you solved a problem in a way that no one else thought was possible. Whether it was fixing a seemingly irreparable error at work, finding a way to support a friend in need from miles away, or helping someone figure out how to make a dream purchase without breaking the bank, journal about the times you tapped into your creative reserves to make the impossible possible.

4. Your Acts of Quiet Courage

   Now it's time to reflect on a personal challenge you faced with silent bravery. Perhaps you ended a toxic relationship, moved cities for a fresh start, sacrificed something you really wanted in order to pay for something someone else really needed, or stood up for what was right despite personal risks. These are the moments of quiet courage that define your character and fortitude. This one might be hard, so take as much time with your pen and journal as you need.

5. The Times You Were Uniquely You

   Having reviewed all those feats of triumph over your life, now celebrate the occasions when being uniquely yourself made all the difference. It could be an instance where your unique perspective or humor brought light to a gloomy situation at work, when you helped a friend going through a financial rough patch, or how your personal touch turned a routine team meeting into an inspiring brainstorm session.

The reason we just dug out these memories from the depths of your memory bank is to really toast the triumphs of your inner underdog, drive home your samurai self, and prove to you that you alone have been enough on many occasions.

But even as we revel in the strength drawn from your past triumphs, it's imperative that we address the profound impact of emotional clutter on your overall well-being and decision-making abilities. Emotional clutter—those unresolved regrets, guilt, and self-reproach that swirl around in our minds—can create turmoil that insidiously affects various aspects of our lives, including financial health. The more this clutter repeats itself, the more it digs in and takes hold until we embrace it for the excuses it gives us to not move forward. We let ourselves believe we're doing fine when all it does is drain our energy. By sorting through this clutter, we can begin to let go of what's not working. We can engage in the act of forgiveness and address these burdens. Forgiving ourselves and showing ourselves a little compassion can improve our levels of self-confidence and self-esteem.[9] We swap negative thoughts for positive ones, lowering our stress levels and freeing up mental space. That allows us to concentrate and focus, enabling us not just to make wiser financial decisions but to foster overall life satisfaction and freedom.

With that, let's move on to the second half of this chapter's exercise, designed to help you confront your emotional clutter with forgiveness and to help you step into your inner power when it comes to how you think about your worth—both literal and metaphorical. On the next page in your journal, create one column to the left labeled "Regrets" and another to the right labeled "Forgiveness."

---

9   Archontia Mantelou and Eirini Karakasidou, "The Effectiveness of a Brief Self-Compassion Intervention Program on Self-Compassion, Positive and Negative Affect and Life Satisfaction," *Psychology* 8, no. 4, (2017), https://doi.org/10.4236/psych.2017.84038.

Begin in the left-hand column, creating a list or writing out full sentences that reflect on your past decisions and actions that continue to evoke discomfort or guilt—these might include personal, professional, or financial regrets. It could be a relationship you mishandled, opportunities you shied away from due to fear, or financial decisions that didn't pan out as hoped. These regrets can linger in your subconscious, subtly influencing your current behaviors and choices across all facets of life. By acknowledging these openly, you initiate the process of emotional decluttering, dismantling the barriers these regrets have erected in your mind.

Dismantling these barriers also translates into rewiring the memory. You begin to remember the lesson, not the perceived failure. If you remember an event as a failure, you instigate negative feelings. If you remember it instead as a lesson, you complete the circuit with a positive ending rather than a negative one.

Then, for each regret, whether personal, professional, or financial, move to the right-hand column and write a statement of forgiveness. This step is about understanding these past actions as integral parts of your growth journey, transforming regret into lessons learned. For instance, forgiving yourself for a failed relationship might be phrased as "I forgive myself for the way that relationship ended. It taught me the importance of communication and honesty in my connections." For a financial regret, it might be "I forgive myself for buying that item that I never used. But it helped me better understand my weakness for a perceived bargain, and I have since learned to recognize when I'm facing FOMO (fear of missing out)." This exercise isn't about excusing your past actions but about recognizing them as stepping stones to a more mature and aware self.

Take a look at the chart you just completed. How does it feel to see this mindset transition on the page? If you're overwhelmed, I get it. It's one thing to say you forgive yourself; it's another thing entirely to actually *feel* that forgiveness, to let the weight of those regrets go, transmuting them into the lessons you need to become that more evolved you.

Consider adopting a physical ritual to symbolically and actually release these regrets. This could involve writing them down on paper and safely burning the paper, or perhaps burying the paper, or releasing it into a flowing river, depending on what feels most cathartic. This ritual represents a clear and intentional break from the past, a commitment to move forward without the emotional clutter that has been subtly influencing your behaviors and self-esteem.

Clearing emotional clutter does more than just free up mental space—it enhances your ability to engage more fully with life. It reduces the cognitive load that these hidden burdens impose, thereby enhancing clarity and emotional energy. In a nutshell, with fewer regrets clouding your judgment, you're better equipped to make decisions that align with your true desires and values, leading to more fulfilling outcomes in all areas of life, including your finances. When you learn to forgive any past indiscretions in your relationship with money, vowing to learn from those mistakes, you can move forward with more confidence. When you understand your own value and how that equates to money, then you are freer to dream, to believe that you are more deserving.

This forgiveness process is crucial for anyone looking to live a more balanced and harmonious life. It's about recognizing and releasing the past, allowing yourself to approach future decisions with a clean slate and a heart unburdened by regret. As we continue our journey, let this renewed sense of liberation infuse your actions and interactions, paving the way for a life truly aligned with your sense of self-worth and potential.

As we conclude this chapter, remember the power of revisiting and celebrating your underdog moments. These are not just past victories; they are the pillars of your future success. They are part of your continuous journey toward financial empowerment and self-worth, where each step you take is built on the knowledge and wisdom gained from the ones before.

Up next, we will delve more deeply into rebuilding your financial landscape with this renewed mindset of worthiness and empowerment. Together, we move forward, not just to earn but to affirm our worth, to claim our "enoughness," and to shape a future where our financial success mirrors our inner value.

CHAPTER 9

PARTY WITH DRUNKEN SAILORS

Your purpose is not to live. Your purpose is to sail.

—MAGELLAN

I hope that you have been able to spend some thoughtful time reflecting on your strengths, your past, and your future since the last chapter, because we're going to continue really working on that sense of self-worth and that money mindset.

But I'm going to take a moment and remind you of this: if you've skimped through the work in these chapters, or if you're just breezing through actually dealing with the tough stuff in this book, remember what happens when you avoid the work—you and your bank account will find yourselves once again at ground zero. If you need to go back and catch up on what we've done thus far, go ahead and do it. I'll wait for you patiently.

So go ahead, make those lists. Burn the pages if you need to. Barbecue those regrets if you haven't yet. It's time to let that shit go!

Just don't also barbecue that list of underdog triumphs that nobody ever thought you'd accomplish. Or your samurai creed. You're going to need those. Because we're going to use those in this chapter as we go partying with drunken sailors. (Don't ask questions—just dive in!)

THE JOURNEY OF LIFE

Have you ever asked yourself what the purpose of life is, for you specifically? Why were you born? And what are you here on earth to do?

Regardless of whatever religion you believe in or philosophy you ascribe to, the whole concept of life and living is really captured by the idea of a journey. It has a beginning, and it has an ending. We start out as babies in the safety of the harbor, and when we are of age, we set sail. We leave the port in our ship destined to go somewhere, intending to arrive at a destination. But it's rarely a linear journey; there are twists and turns and sidetracks all along the way.

If you haven't read Homer's *Odyssey*, it's a lot like that. In this epic poem, the main character, King Odysseus, wanders for ten years trying to get home to his wife, Penelope, and son Telemachus after spending ten years fighting the Trojan War. He has a clear starting point and destination, but he has a heck of a time getting there.

He is taken captive by the goddess Calypso, is bombarded by trials from Poseidon, shipwrecks, narrowly escapes the Cyclops, shipwrecks again, deals with lazy and greedy crewmen, travels to the underworld, is helped by the goddess Athena, and finally has to kill more than a hundred men who have taken over his home while he was gone.

He literally has to travel to hell and back before he can fully complete his journey and live happily ever after.

Just like Odysseus, our real-life journey always turns out to be more of an odyssey than anything else (and now we know where the word *odyssey* comes from!). We end up taking detours, scenic (and not-so-scenic) routes, and bypasses to get around obstacles in our way.

In a sense, this journey is like getting drunk and letting some other drunken sailor take charge of our ship. They come along and take the wheel while we sit back and let them guide our journey wherever they think we need to go. It doesn't mean we're lost or that the journey is over. It just means we're going in a different direction.

These drunken sailors might be parents, boyfriends or girlfriends, well-meaning mentors, or friends. We just end up giving them total control of our ship, and before we know it, we're fighting a cyclops, hearing sirens, facing horrible monsters, and generally going completely off course. Hopefully, we become wiser and stronger for all this, but those detours are not taking us where we should be going. And they've consumed a lot of our all-too-precious time—time we could have been spending on something more productive and far more profitable to our self-worth and our bank account.

So I ask you now: Who have you been letting steer your ship? Why have you let these drunken sailors take charge of your vessel? And how can we walk them off the plank? It's time to get your ship together!

Take out a blank piece of paper, and draw a little ship. I don't care what kind. It doesn't have to be fancy, but it needs to represent your boat. Maybe it's a rowboat or a yacht or a cargo ship. You get to choose this adventure because you're the captain of the ship. Imagine this ship is fully stocked with food, fuel, and all the provisions it needs to support you for the rest of your life. Define your destination: Is it some past event where something didn't go quite as planned? Something you want to course-correct and reimagine a successful outcome? Maybe it's a goal you have not yet met? Add this label to the drawing in front of that ship. Now, before you set off, go ahead and draw seven sailors aboard your boat. We'll come back to those guys in a moment. And don't draw yourself yet. Pretend you're in the ship's cabin if you need to. But don't worry—we'll come back to your role in this journey soon too.

Let's say you were leaving Santiago, Chile, to go to Easter Island. That's the plan. But after you leave shore, those seven sailors you're traveling with start tossing back the booze. The party is in full swing, and you're on drink number [redacted—a lady never boats, boozes, and tells] when you realize you've somehow ended up in Fiji. You're now completely off course. Not that there's anything wrong with Fiji; it just wasn't where you were wanting to go. Your sailors got the better of you, and you have lost control of yourself and your ship. At this point, you don't feel a stronger sense of self-worth, and your bank account is no better off than when you started the journey.

Now that you realize you are so far off course, it's time to identify and give a name to the culprit, all the drunken sailors that caused you to detour. Was it a person, an event, an obsession, a distraction? For many, the sailors manifest in an anxiety over other people's opinions. You thought letting someone else helm the ship for a brief time would somehow make you a worthier person, completely ignoring the journey that you were on—a journey that, let's face it, you may have just begun in the wake of the last load of drunken sailors.

The drunken sailors run on our emotions, including fear of abandonment, missing self-esteem, or codependency. Maybe your sailor was a new interest or a talent you discovered. Maybe it was a religion or a philosophy you got obsessed with. Maybe it was a romantic interest that took you where you didn't intend to go. Maybe it was changing majors or careers or locations because someone said it would be good for you. Or maybe you were a victim of circumstances out of your control.

> Take all the time you need to reflect on your life, and then above each of the seven sailors you drew, give them a name. Label every force that has taken you off course. And if you run out of names before all seven sailors have one, might I gently suggest that you're lying to yourself. Maybe go back to any unfinished exercises from earlier in the book and then come back and take a good hard look at your crew.

Once you've identified your drunken sailors, ask yourself this: "How did I lose myself this much?" You wasted so much time and energy on this person or situation that didn't deserve to take that much out of you—and remember, time is money. Time is all we have—it's your most valuable asset, and understanding that is a big part of understanding your self-worth. These sailors sucked all the energy out of you, and now, in hindsight, you can realize the shitshow they made of your journey. It's time to see these sailors for who they are now—one big descanso on the roadside. The party has been your demise, and now you're hungover.

But why? Why did you hand the wheel over in the first place?

Now, I want you to list the one reason this drunken yacht party got so out of hand. Carefully consider at what point you knew that you'd gone down the wrong path a little too far. When you reached that point, something clicked and made you realize you were chasing pipe dreams. What was that moment? And can you trace it back to the moment you started down this unintended path in the first place?

You have to get rid of some of these drunken sailors before they derail you any further. Make them walk the plank. Well, not all of them, of course. An unexpected pregnancy may have brought an unplanned detour, but it likely became one of life's greatest blessings, with your child now being an irreplaceable part of your journey.. But you have to get rid of the toxic sailors, and you can't do this until you figure out how they got control of you in the first place.

You might need to flip your journal's page over for this next part of the exercise, but now that you identified the singular reason you went off course, it's now time to look again at those seven drunken sailors and for each one list any and every reason they had control over you. What was it about them that convinced you to hand over your autonomy and let them steer?

One woman I worked with spent decades going from one bad relationship to another until she found herself nearly forty and still single. Her desperation for a relationship brought her to marry a man who derailed her career. Another woman let her ambitions for a better job get in the way of what she actually wanted to do with her life. There are as many reasons for our detours as there are grains of sand in the sea. What are yours?

Armed with the knowledge of who your drunken sailors are and why and how you got here, now you can take back control of your ship. I want you to draw yourself at the helm of your ship. It can be a stick figure if you want; it doesn't matter. But it should symbolize you as the master of your own journey now. You know the "Invictus" quote, by William Ernest Henley: "I am the master of my fate. I am the captain of my soul"? You are now the master and captain of your life.

Next, I want to ask you to encapsulate the whole experience you have just had throughout this exercise in a single word or one emotion. Is it *resilience*? *Tolerance*? *Acceptance*? *Vigilance*? Pull out a thesaurus if you have to, but write that one word large and in charge directly over your stick figure's head. Then turn the page, because you're going to take that one word and expand it into a paragraph, starting with this one sentence:

"My journey thus far has been epic, because it has taught me [your word here]."

> Keep writing about what you've learned and what your selected word means to you until you've written at least five more sentences.
>
> Now that you know what you've learned from where you've been, it's time to get to where you're going. Start a new paragraph, and begin by redefining your journey with this first sentence:
>
> "I will know I have successfully arrived at my destination when ... "

This should be the ultimate, most grand version of you that you could ever imagine. Where do you picture yourself living in your wildest imagination? What are you wearing? What are you driving? What are you doing with your time? What is your profession? How much money are you making? And who are the people in your life?

Be as specific as you possibly can be about that big, crazy, ambitious goal that you have deep in your mind, remembering that you are worth it! You are an absolute masterpiece, and you will get what you deserve one day. You are so absurdly worthy it should bring you to tears.

As for me, I learned many years ago that I am meant to thrive, and my purpose on earth is to help other women thrive as well. I was born to change the lives of millions of women, and since realizing this, I have seen them make hundreds of millions of dollars because they knew their destination.

I know this isn't going to be a guarantee. There will still be detours and obstacles, but you can preempt many of them by holding true to your course and not handing over the wheel. You can be vigilant for those red flags that always come before disaster and take matters into your own hands, whether you avoid them, confront them, or change them into something different. *Now* you can let people back onto your ship, but only the kinds of people who will not hijack your journey.

On your next journal page, draw your boat again. This time I want you to choose at least five reliable sailors who you want to have aboard with you. As you write their names above their heads, ask yourself why you want them on your crew, and then write those reasons down too. Maybe they will help you make better decisions or help you move faster. Maybe they can point out the toxic influences that you still can't see. For whatever reason, they must add value to your journey, and you get to decide exactly what that means.

You may still deviate from your course a little, but you'll be able to get back on track much more quickly when you have the right crew. Add as many new crew members as you want.

Finally, it's time to pack your bags. What are you absolutely taking on your new journey? Complete this sentence in your journal:

"I am bringing with me ..."

What are the tools you always need so that you can captain this ship to your dream paradise island? We all have tools that help us stay on track, including things like our savings, our mindfulness practices, our belief systems, our talents, and our character. What is it that you know you will rely on for the rest of your life to get you to that goal?

If you look back at your life so far and notice the path veering all over the map, I don't want you to despair. All is not lost. In fact, everything is actually very, very right. The journey is what has made you *you*!

I would argue that Odysseus was probably a much better king after he got home than he had been before he left for the Trojan War. Had he not learned everything that he learned, had he not survived everything that he survived, he wouldn't have come home as grateful as he did. He was able to stand in absolute awe and gratitude of this woman and son who were both still waiting for him.

There's contrast to everything that we do. All of the bad shit that does happen to us brings this contrast to us. All of those monsters that we face—such as, in my case, my brother's death—everything that happens to us comes with the opportunity for us to make it either a lesson or an opportunity for change. You can just choose to ignore it or learn from it. It's a matter of looking at it with the right perspective.

Steve Jobs gave a commencement address at Stanford in 2005 that has been widely distributed and quoted. In it, he shared a story about his personal odyssey during his early days at Reed College. We all know he dropped out of college because he couldn't justify the expense and what he felt was the waste of time learning things he didn't feel he needed to know. Rather than going home, he stayed on campus and decided to take a class in calligraphy after noticing that every poster and drawer label was beautifully hand calligraphed, and he talked about that in the address:[10]

> ... I learned about serif and sans serif typefaces, about varying the amount of space between different letter combinations, about what makes great typography great. It was

---

10   "'You've Got to Find What You Love,' Jobs Says," StanfordReport, June 12, 2005, https://news.stanford.edu/stories/2005/06/youve-got-find-love-jobs-says.

beautiful, historical, artistically subtle in a way that science can't capture, and I found it fascinating.

None of this had even a hope of any practical application in my life. But 10 years later, when we were designing the first Macintosh computer, it all came back to me. And we designed it all into the Mac.… If I had never dropped in on that single course in college, the Mac would have never had multiple typefaces or proportionally spaced fonts. And since Windows just copied the Mac, it's likely that no personal computer would have them.… you can't connect the dots looking forward; you can only connect them looking backward. So you have to trust that the dots will somehow connect in your future. You have to trust in something—your gut, destiny, life, karma, whatever. This approach has never let me down, and it has made all the difference in my life.

Life is meant to be lived. Author and self-described "philosophical entertainer" Alan Watts spent much of his adult life encouraging people to find joy in every moment of life. In the 1960s and 1970s, he was one of the first people to integrate the spiritual teachings from Buddhist, Taoist, and Hindu teachings and share them with Western audiences who were largely unaware of them at the time. In one of his lectures, he shares that life is a dance. I encourage you to read his complete thoughts online, but am sharing some particularly striking points from his discussion here:[11]

> … the physical universe, is basically playful.… it doesn't have some destination that it ought to arrive at. But it is best

---

11   Alan Watts, "The Tao of Philosophy (Part 1)," Alan Watts Organization, accessed July 2024, https://alanwatts.org/transcripts/the-tao-of-philosophy/.

understood by analogy with music. Because music as an art form is essentially playful; we say "you play the piano," you don't work the piano.

… Music differs from say, travel. When you travel, you are trying to get somewhere.… In music though, one doesn't make the end of a composition the point of the composition. If that were so … there would be composers who wrote only finales.… Same way with dancing.… The whole point of the dancing is the dance.

… We've got a system of schooling which gives a completely different impression.… now you go to kindergarten … when you finish that you get into first grade … and then you get out of grade school and you go to high school … then you're going to go to college … and when you're through with graduate school you go out to join the World.… And all the time this thing is coming.… the success you're working for. Then, when you wake up one day—about 40 years old—you say, "My God, I've arrived! …" … And there's a slight let-down because you feel there's a … dreadful hoax. Look at the people who live to retire and … then, when they're 65, they don't have any energy left, they're more or less impotent, and they go and rot in an old people's … community.… We thought of life by analogy with a journey … which had a serious purpose at the end, and the thing was to get to that end.… But we missed the point the whole way along. It was a musical thing and you were supposed to sing, or to dance, while the music was being played.…

My friend, this is where the magic starts happening. This is where the dolphins start jumping over your ship as you sail toward those powder-white beaches full of coconuts and mangoes. In spite of all the chaos involved, you have finally heaved the drunken sailors overboard because they never knew how to really dance with you anyway. Ascribe to them a single descanso on the roadside, and then move on. You have now chosen the path less traveled and all that comes with it—the wealth, the success, the truthful feelings of self-worth. This is where your self-worth turns into the adventure of a lifetime that manifests in success beyond your wildest dreams. This is where you now focus on the power inside you and begin the new you with habits that reflect those of the most successful people. You now know you are worthy of more, and you are ready to claim that bountiful treasure. This is the reason you are on this journey in the first place!

CHAPTER 10

THE TSUNAMI WARNING

If you were born with the weakness to fail, you
were born with the strength to rise.
—RUPI KAUR

Congratulations on getting a grip on your life! You have been through storms and seen monsters and slain dragons. It sure looks like smooth sailing ahead from now on, doesn't it?

Okay, let's get real. You know as well as I do that this isn't going to be the end of the story. Life just isn't that simple.

But before we get any further, I have to warn you. Things are going to take a somber turn. Honestly, this chapter is probably going to be the hardest to read in the whole book, both emotionally and mentally. If you take it seriously and complete your next mission with solemn intent, there's a pretty good chance you will feel triggered to some degree. To make it even more clear, we are going to get into some really deep shit here.

I invite you up front to check in with yourself. What's coming is not for the fainthearted. Are you ready to dig deep and do something really, really hard? Do you feel emotionally stable enough to have a hard look at your mortality and come out the other side? This stuff isn't for the faint of heart, but I promise you, it is a critical part of your journey to self-worth, which will lead to greater ease, confidence, and ultimately success in all realms of life.

I also invite you to trust me here, more than you have before. I have been on this journey too, and I have seen women just like you come out the other side of this in a much better space than when they started. They are more confident in their purpose and able to command respect like never before. It does get better.

In short, things are going to get pretty hairy, but it's worth it!

Before you read this, I want you to prepare physically for what you are about to do. The rest of this chapter is best done in one sitting, so I suggest waiting until you have an uninterrupted hour or more to continue reading. When you have set that time aside, make sure your journal is handy with your favorite pen. Put yourself in a place where you can do some serious reflecting.

Ready? Let's begin.

THE CLOCK IS TICKING

Now that you're rid of your drunken sailors, you're happily sailing on your ship. Let's imagine you are enjoying that magnificent expanse of deep ocean in the Pacific. Picture yourself there. There is no land in sight. The sun is bright. Puffy white clouds dot the blue sky. Dolphins and sea turtles occasionally rise out of the water around your boat. Joyful little fish nibble at the algae that has collected on the sides. Life is good. So good.

And then you get an emergency radio call. The International Maritime Authority rings you and says, "We need to let you know that the largest earthquake ever recorded just happened off the coast of South America. The Nazca tectonic plates have shifted like they've never shifted in recorded history. A gigantic oceanic convulsion of magnitudes never experienced is heading your way. We've never seen anything like it before. Prepare for the worst. We project that you have roughly five hours. To be honest, you're not going to make it out alive. This is the time to set your affairs in order, and the clock is ticking. Over and out."

Take a moment to read those words again. Repeat them out loud if you want to let them sink in as if they were real. You have five hours or less before your life is over.

Get your journal out. Set a timer for ten minutes, and let the pen guide you as you process what you are feeling. Consider the following questions:

- Who do you need to forgive?
- Who do you need to thank?
- Who do you need to call?
- What conversations do you need to have over these next five hours?
- What do you need to say in those conversations?
- Who do you need to tell to f*ck off because of all the pain they've inflicted?
- What anger do you need to let go of?
- Are there any other affairs you need to set in order before you die?

> Again, I encourage you to take this seriously. Write down every thought, impression, and emotion you have. Don't worry if it's a jumbled mess. There is no right or wrong way to do this. The important thing is that you be as real and raw as you can on the page.

When I did this the first time, I bawled my eyes out. This is supposed to touch a nerve, so if you need to grab a box of tissues, that's okay!

One of the women who did this activity in one of my workshops discovered in the end that she had essentially written a love letter to her family and neighbors and a hate letter to her boss.

Another woman discovered at this step that she held on to a lot more resentment than she realized. This is what she wrote: "It doesn't make sense to be angry at anyone in this world. You have only this one life, and letting anyone come into your life who makes you angry is such a waste. I don't want to be angry anymore." She realized that she had been unconsciously holding grudges against her children, her spouse, her coworkers, and many others, and this was holding her back from embracing the wholehearted connections that she craved. (By the way, I am not a therapist. I don't ever claim to be able to fix those kinds of deep-seated issues, but as they say, self-awareness is the first step!)

Now, if you think I'm a jerk for doing this to you, I beg your forgiveness. But I am not going to stop there. Stick with me and take a deep breath, because we're about to get a little darker.

We are fast-forwarding several weeks, and the search party has discovered the remains of your ship after the tsunami wiped it out. They find the captain's journal you kept and the black box that recorded everything that happened during the tsunami. The head of the search party starts reading your journal from page one, and they start to see the plans you had written in your log prior to hearing that fateful alert. They piece together your plans for the journey and the intended goals you had set out to achieve.

> Turn to a fresh page in your journal and write down all the things that were yet to be accomplished in your intended journey. There are no do-overs here. You're dead and buried at sea. Now, answer the following questions and any others that come to mind as you write:
>
> - What dreams were left undone?
> - How much money were you meant to make?
> - How were you supposed to change the world?
> - What was that job?
> - What was the masterpiece you were supposed to reveal to the world that you didn't?
> - What was your legacy?
> - What was your life supposed to be like?

One woman I did this with said, "I wanted to be at peace with myself. I set out on the journey to remove the masks I wore to fit in with society and become the best version of myself. I wanted to travel the world and discover my artistic side."

Your answers might be similar to hers.

Another woman wrote, "I didn't become the president of the United States." She told the group that she felt ridiculous for journaling that, which broke my heart. Why should she apologize for that? She shouldn't! Even if she had "only" gone into law or politics, she would have been closer to her goal. Who knows? Maybe she would have become a mayor or a governor or the president of a company if she hadn't stomped on her ambition.

Thankfully this is all make-believe, but I encourage you to really dig deep. Are there regrets you can anticipate having if it were real?

Now that you see your dreams more clearly, let's say you have a time machine—but not one where you can go back and live in the past. This time machine can only be used to send messages back in time. You have one shot to send a letter to yourself—a message in a bottle, if you will.

Turn to another fresh page in your journal, and answer this one question:

- What do you tell your past captain-self back at the start of the journey to help her actually accomplish those dreams?

This might feel a little bit like self-flagellation, but bear with me. Consider your big, crazy goals, and think of how you could have made different choices so you would be more spiritually, emotionally, and physically healthy. What advice are you giving yourself in the past?

Perhaps you tell yourself to begin self-publishing your poetry in high school so that your dream of becoming a famous poet can actually happen. Maybe that would have led to changing lives for the better and being able to afford that dream wedding you never got?

Maybe you needed to take your health risks more seriously when you were young and have taken better care of your body so you didn't deteriorate into illness?

Or maybe it's as simple as standing up for yourself to your first boss so you would be recognized for the value you added. If you had done this, you would have begun moving up in your company sooner and would have been compensated for your worth, not your title.

Once that's done, I want to suggest that you sit with it for a minute. Clearly, we can't go back and change time. But there's a difference between hoping that something would have happened and actually making it happen. You can't wish or dream or hope your way to making things happen. Obviously that hasn't worked, or you would've done it by now.

Take a moment to think about yourself right now as that past captain of the ship and consider what you might need to hear today from your future self. Now, answer the following question in your journal:

- What does your future successful self want to say to your present self?

Be as specific as you can. Declaring what will happen and how to get there opens you up to the possibility that your dreams actually can come true. You can map out all the hows to get the life you want. There are millions of different hows, but they have to be an energetic match. Don't say you are going to own a company if you aren't interested

> in business. Consider who you are deep inside and where your soul wants to go. Then write that down too.

That is the last writing activity I am going to ask you to do in this chapter. It's time to put the pen down and go get a drink of water. Crying sure makes a body dehydrated!

While you do that, I'm going to share a secret with you. There are two people whom I confer with on many of my business problems. You are going to think I'm freaking crazy, but it works wonders. These two mentors are Mother Teresa and Steve Jobs. Sure, they are long gone, but I have imaginary conversations with both of them when I'm going to sleep.

I'll say, "MT, I need to solve this problem. I know you're going to help me figure out the solution by tomorrow morning. Thank you."

Boom. Next morning, I have the answer.

It's not like I suddenly have a vision of Mother Teresa or anything. But I allow my subconscious mind to ponder on what this wonderful lady would do if she were in my situation. Or what Steve would tell me if he were sitting next to me. Sometimes I have an imaginary conversation, which I know sounds completely illogical and crazy, but I do it anyway. Having a mentor, even an imaginary one, can make a world of difference!

I have said this before, but it bears repeating: The reticular activating system in your brain is in charge of attracting all evidence that supports your belief. Like when I wanted a Tesla, I suddenly started noticing Teslas everywhere. Then I found out the down payment wasn't all that bad, and next thing I know, I've never been happier driving than when I drive my Tesla. Same with getting my whole family front-row tickets to see Taylor Swift in Europe. I visualized being delighted by bringing my whole family to hang out with Taylor in Europe, just reveling in how much we were enjoying our time there. Then I let that thought go. And guess what? I was easily able to afford to take my whole family, my mother, and a friend to see Taylor Swift, front row, in Munich, at her biggest concert to date on that tour. To top it off, my kids each received one of her guitar picks!

It's been proven that if you fantasize or visualize a successful outcome to the goal you ultimately want, you're more likely to get there, because it raises the serotonin in your brain, which makes you happy. And a happy state is more likely to attract what you want than an unhappy state.[12]

The story you're telling yourself is that you're not worthy of your ambitions. But is it actually true that you're not worthy of them? Life did not set you up with big, hairy, ambitious goals and dreams to leave them unaccomplished. Or to leave you unpaid, for that matter. Your creator, whoever that might be, did not endow you with such vast ambition to leave it just sitting there.

There's a reason, for example, that my dream was not to become a football player, and it never was. Why? Because it's just not within my realm of possibilities to ever do that. But your dreams? They're there for a reason. And if you weren't worthy, you wouldn't have them. They wouldn't be yours. You wouldn't even think of them as your dream.

What would it feel like for you to be that woman who's already normalized having shitloads of money? Who's already normalized having the successful book, the business, the career, the CEO role? Normalize that, and *feel* it. What does it feel like to make $15,000 a

---

12   Tchiki Davis, "How Visualization Can Benefit Your Well-Being," Psychology Today (blog), November 20, 2023, https://www.psychologytoday.com/intl/blog/click-here-for-happiness/202308/how-visualization-can-benefit-your-well-being.

month? What would you spend it on? How would you use that money to benefit yourself, your loved ones, and your community?

I assure you that you are worth every penny you want and more.

The key is to understand the word *normalizing*. Make it feel like daily happenstance. Not foreign. I remember how quickly my net worth began increasing when this clicked for me. You start with small baby steps of what you can expect each month. Then normalize the sources of revenue. Normalize the idea of you earning an income from your job and multiple other revenue streams. Normalize the idea of *you* owning real estate, book royalties, an online business, buying houses in other countries, etc. Normalize the idea of you having a huge tax bill at the end of the year, and wear that tax bracket as a badge of honor.

That was one mother-trucking experience, wasn't it? Good job. Pat yourself on the back. I'm so proud of everything you are doing. You've come so far! Thank you for allowing me to be part of this journey. You have no idea how powerful this is for me and for my own journey. So again, I thank you.

Now that I hope you have become more comfortable with the idea that you are not just worth more but also deserve more, let's home in on those thoughts and really dig into what money means to you.

PART III

CATCH THE DREAM WAVE

We've reflected on all the things that have held you back and journaled ways to understand and rebuild a sense of self. It's been, let's face it, exhausting—but also exhilarating. Now that you're on a firmer footing, we're going to spend the last two chapters delving into your relationship with money and just how far your dreams can take you. Like a surfer's dream wave that we're watching roll in over the horizon, these last two chapters will help you feel the momentum coming in and let you see how prepared you are to know when it's time to jump on the surfboard and ride the wave.

CHAPTER 11

YOU CAN'T GET THERE FROM HERE

You can only become truly accomplished at something you love. Don't make money your goal. Instead, pursue the things you love doing, and then do them so well that people can't take their eyes off you.
—MAYA ANGELOU

Those last couple of chapters were kind of heavy, weren't they? Well, thankfully that tsunami never happened. You weren't lost at sea, and you didn't really have to consider how you would spend your last moments.

I hope you took the activities seriously enough, though, that you've gained a new perspective on life. What if you were literally given a new lease on life, exactly in this moment? What would you be doing differently in terms of financial beliefs and choices?

Listen, I get it. There's a prevailing feeling among many women in our society that being tied to money is always a negative thing. We chose not to be wealthy because money is evil. Look at all the villains in fairy tales and movies. Wicked stepmothers are often queens wearing gold and jewels. The "bad guy" is usually a penny-pinching rich man or woman. In reality, we vilify people like Kim Kardashian. If they're really rich, that must mean they're really bad people. If I say the word *billionaire*, do you picture someone recklessly jetting around the world without an ounce of care for other people?

I know you know that there really are good people out there who have money and are amazing souls. Mother Teresa flew around in her private jet not because she wanted to show everyone that she had all the money in the world but because it made it easier for her to fulfill her purpose. Money is a tool to achieve purpose.

Money should be a refinery, not a curse. I believe there is absolutely nothing accidental about the path you're taking right now or about the way you're growing as a human being. When you have money, the process of becoming who you are gets a little bit easier. But it doesn't make the tragedies or hardships of life go away. I'm a firm believer that absolutely everybody has been brought up and forged in the same way that pearls are forged. It all starts with a speck of dirt that gets into the oyster and irritates it. You have been irritated your entire life to become who you are becoming.

It is my most sincere opinion that when you have money, it is a little bit easier to be who you were always meant to be. By being alive, we all have to go through challenges. Believe me, I know this. I mean, at this point 50 percent of my family has died on me, and all sorts of tragedies have happened, but I have been able to sustain my purpose. I've understood that when I live from a place of feeling that I am worthy of my purpose and that my purpose is a worthy pursuit, money shows up and accelerates my progress toward doing and being more of what I love. Money has been here to help me create the reality that I want. It's a catalyst for my enjoyment and my purpose; it helps me make the differences in the world that I want to make. And it can do the same for you.

INHERITED MONEY MINDSET

It's very common for women to see money flow—it comes in, and it goes out. We get paychecks just to turn around and write checks to pay bills. Money is not traditionally associated with a feminine energy. To compound the difficulty in making and saving money, there are some stories we heard growing up.

Let's unpack the conversations you heard around the dinner table and try to better understand how you've inherited certain perspectives around money. What did you hear your parents say about money? How did their attitudes define your relationship with money? What beliefs about money did you inherit?

My dad was savvy at investing and saving for our future. I watched him always finding ways to save and grow his money. Mom was always very money savvy as well, but her belief tended more toward "You can't take it to your grave, so you might as well spend it." I noticed she tended not to want to touch money much, though. She'd rather give it to someone to invest, give it away, or spend it on others to make them happy.

Growing up, I kind of liked my mom's approach and subconsciously blocked my dad's, because for me, it was not logical to wait months to get a bike. I thought we could just get a cheap bike so we wouldn't have to wait. At the time, I didn't understand the value of things the way my father did.

To make things more complicated, at some point I was given the message that I was not good at saving money. I honestly don't know where that came from, but I remember feeling that I was not responsible or trustworthy enough with money, so why bother trying to save it for something in the future? I've had to work hard to overcome some of these limiting beliefs.

While working with women, I found out all kinds of reasons they were holding themselves back, and a majority of these were learned in their youth. Maybe they felt they were a financial burden on their parents, which in turn instilled a belief that having a family of their own would be a financial burden. Children and pets cost a lot, so they believed they couldn't set financial goals beyond keeping a roof over their heads and their bellies full.

I also worked with women who inherited a philosophy that they didn't belong in the workplace at all. The conversations they heard from their parents and other adults were about girls needing to stay in their place. They were told girls should desire nothing more than being a wife and mother, and these messages sank deep.

Other women were never told as young girls that they were valuable, which resulted in their undervaluing themselves in the workplace. They never thought to ask for more money because they had an unconscious belief that they were not as valuable as other employees. It took a quantum leap for them to start thinking of asking for a raise or increasing the rates they charged for services.

Of course, there are less corrosive money mentalities that hold us back. Many women I know were raised in homes where money just wasn't a goal. They grew into women who were not motivated by money. Sure, they wanted to be comfortable, but they never set lofty financial goals and certainly never dreamed of luxury.

It's hard to heal when in your head you've still got your dad telling you at the dinner table that rich people aren't good. And becoming rich would make you like "them." That women shouldn't be making money. Your adult brain knows that none of these things are actually true, yet you still sometimes find yourself making decisions based on these things. Your dad is probably freaking proud that you're making all this money and that you're changing the role model for women in the future. But in our heads, the stories we tell ourselves keep us under these proverbial glass ceilings. Our subconscious beliefs become our roadblocks.

Another woman, Patty, told me in one of our sessions that her inherited money mindset had been holding her back from putting in for a promotion: "I had an opportunity to renegotiate my position with my boss, and once I began to see what I was worth, I began advocating for myself more. They doubled my salary without hesitation. I walked out of the office thinking, *Gee, I should have asked for more. I just asked for a double, but I'll bet they would have gone even higher if I would have asked!* I worked on a plan for my professional growth, and they offered me a promotion a short time later. I just did not even know that could be possible before, because I never thought that I could put myself forward like that. Now I know my worth, and others know it too."

This is where we have to learn to get out of our own way!

STOP THINKING LINEARLY

When I tell you to stop thinking linearly, what do you think I mean? Are you suddenly back in high school geometry class and picturing lines with arrows at each end? In a way, that's actually kind of what I'm talking about.

We're trained to think that life happens on a continuous line. You go through school, you go to college, you go to work, you start a family. You do things in the way that the super-responsible you would do them, right? You save your money so that perhaps by year thirty of your career, you've got enough in your savings and 401(k) to retire and do things in a safe way. Which is not to say that it is wrong.

But earning potential is not a linear thing. Intrinsic value doesn't follow a career track. Confidence and creativity don't fall in a straight line, and as a result, there are endless ways in which you can always increase your earning potential. Revenue streams can flow like rivers, continuous, winding, ever flowing, and simultaneous. They are always present and always accessible, meaning you don't have to reach a certain step in your life to get more.

If you said today, "I want to generate an extra $15,000 a month, and I'm going to set my mind on this," you have everything you need within you to do that. You are creative. You are valuable. You are capable. Remember, if you can envision it, you are already equipped with everything required to achieve that vision. All you need is the belief and certainty that comes from knowing at your core that you are worthy enough to pursue your vision.

It is just mind blowing when you truly realize that who you've always been and who you will always be is a freaking masterpiece. Your creator (whoever you believe that to be) endowed you with those dreams of earning a bucketload of money or creating whatever it is that you want to create out of your life. Why would that be the case if he or she or it didn't also endow you with absolutely every last tool or resource to get you there? Decide that you are enough. Decide that you are fit to be queen.

It's an adventure, but you have a lot more power than you give yourself credit for. You're a much more powerful creator than what time limits you to be. Does that make sense? I know this seems a little out there, but it really is true. Thinking of time in a linear fashion is limiting. Too many people go through life thinking you are born and then you die, so keep your head down and suffer through it. This prevents you from realizing everything you've created up until now, who you've become, and the beautiful path you took to get where you are today.

There is a common philosophical question that you may have heard: "Do we, as humans, really have free will?"

This is often explained with the analogy of a tree. If we know that a tree starts from a seed and grows with water, sun, and air, it has no choice about what it will become. Sure, the leaves will fall off, but they fall off because the air has turned cold and the tree quits nourishing them and pulls the sap deep into its trunk, so they become brittle and fall. This discussion then turns to humans. In life, do we ever choose for ourselves, or will we always do the same because of what we are and what our environment is?

I would argue that humans are not like trees. We have much more control over the outcomes of our choices than we realize. If you think about it, there have probably been a lot of instances in your life when you focused enough energy and enough attention on a particular topic and shit happened way faster than it was supposed to happen. This is what I'm talking about. Focus your energy and your time on those dreams.

Close your eyes for just a moment, and imagine your bank account has an extra $50,000 in it. After you get over the jittery excitement of having this extra cash, what's the first thing you would do with it? Do you want to save it or get rid of it? Would you pay off a loan? Make an extra mortgage payment?

Now imagine that amount is suddenly $100,000. What do you do? Are you immediately planning a bucket list vacation? Thinking of going back to school? Maybe helping friends or family or even donating it to a cause you are passionate about? Maybe you think about investing some of it for the future?

Okay, one more. Let's move that up to $1 million. What do you feel as you imagine this amount suddenly coming into your bank account—no strings attached. One freaking *million* dollars. What do you feel when you picture that number popping up in your account? Is there a feeling of nervousness? Of fear, even? That amount of money comes with a weight.

I have noticed that most everyone has some degree of three different personas as it relates to handling money:

1. **The super-responsible one:** This woman invests that $1 million and lives moderately. She may lose some of the money because of the market, but she's doing what she's "supposed" to do with the money. She is the CEO type with a diversified portfolio and an understanding of compounding interest. You might see her in a designer gown once for a gala, but otherwise she's practical as shit. She uses money to create a sense of control and safety in her life and to improve her status. This person is driven by external validation.

2. **The super-reckless one:** She parties away all that money and, by the end of year one, has nothing. She's the one who wants to show the world that she flies around in her private jet. She is so cool and has all the frivolous things we know very rich people have—the statues of giant kitty-cats for $100,000 and insanely expensive shoes she never takes out of the box. She hosts parties and takes all her friends with her to Fashion Week. She uses money to be more accepted and loved. This person is driven by external validation, but a different kind—obviously.

3. **The super-authentic one:** She just truly follows her heart, does with it what she feels called to do, and understands

that money can be a catalyst for great things personally and externally. She knows money is a tool for a better life and a better world and that there is no limit to how much she is allowed to have. She uses it to benefit herself and the things she cares about. This person is driven by internal validation.

These versions of you play the game simultaneously, vying for the steering wheel every time we make a financial decision. Let's face it, it'd be quite hard to be in the driver's seat aiming for a destination if you're constantly shifting between Jekyll and Hyde.

And making it even worse are all the other influences that come into play. What does society say is the right thing for you to do with your money? Are you supposed to take it and make it grow in a safe way? Maybe buy a couple of real estate properties, put it in the bank, invest. Are you supposed to be investing in stocks and bonds, and if so, how much? Are you supposed to be contributing to social causes and charities you support? Do you need to tithe? What about your kids and grandkids in the future? Don't they deserve some of it? How much is the world you live in expecting you to give away?

Then think of your inherited money stories. What would your parents advise you to do around the dinner table? What does that little-girl version of you think is right? Are you supposed to hand it over to someone else who knows how to manage it because money's a dirty word? Do you feel like you should hand it over to a man in a suit and tie and cuff links who knows better so that it's outta sight, outta mind?

And what do you get out of this whole thing, anyway? Even if you're usually the super-responsible one putting your money in the bank, that doesn't make *you* worthier. Sure, it makes your assets potentially grow a little bit, but your asset is not the money or anything you do with it. It's you.

In one of my workshops, a woman shared her experience with this principle in the early stages of her journey:

> I didn't have a million dollars fall into my bank account, but my husband and I had some savings in our account, and I knew it was time for me to quit my dead-end job and find something better. This gave me the freedom to look at what I was doing, begin taking all the classes, doing all the research, and making all the plans on how to have a successful business of my own. I thought hard on what my business model should be and what I personally needed to do to get there. I taught myself how to set up a good website. I spent all my time self-investing, and now I'm mentally five times as happy as I was. And even though I've just barely started my company, I'm not far off from matching my salary from before. I'm well on my way to realizing my dream revenue.

The only way you can grow as an asset yourself, and to ensure you are worthy of even more money and more dreams and more ambitions, is if you work on yourself. It really comes down to normalizing a heightened sense of worthiness. When you feel worthy, you do great work. When you do great work, your work commands more money. More money inspires you to do even greater work. Which begs this question: What do you think has held you back until now from doing your greatest work? Why are you not there yet?

Going back to that same Stanford University commencement speech by Steve Jobs (if you haven't yet, you should go check it out on YouTube), here's a quote that drives home my point above: "Your work is going to fill a large part of your life, and the only way to be truly satisfied is to do what you believe is great work. And the only way to do great work is to love what you do. If you haven't found it yet, keep looking. Don't settle. As with all matters of the heart, you'll know when you find it."

The only limiting factor between a four-figure salary and a six- or seven-figure salary is your ability to normalize it. It's about how much we think we're capable of making. Before you start making excuses, I'm going to stop you. It's really never the market, but we think it's the market. It's not the lack of job opportunities. It's not the gaps in our résumé. Or the competition. We think it's all these things. But we're wrong!

It's time to try to sort out some of these tangled relationships in yourself. Write this down:

- Why am I not financially where I want to be?

Now take five minutes to answer that. Don't censor yourself. Just write down every single factor and limiting belief that comes to you in terms of your financial restrictions.

Now make three columns to represent the three main ways we have been taught to relate to money: "Super-responsible me," "Super-reckless me," and "Super-authentic me." (Remember, hypothetically, you've just received that $1 million I mentioned a few pages ago.)

In the first two columns, write down what you would do if (1) this were real and (2) you were to fully be in that mindset for the rest of your life. Are you purchasing a ranch in Wyoming? Are you investing in the stock market? Are you putting it away for your kids? Have fun with this, and think big!

Then look at the third column. How do you use money to expand *you?* How do you use your wealth to grow yourself toward your purpose and move closer to that greater version of you that you've always wanted to be? In this column, you get permission to ignore the rest of the world around you and just use it to grow you. No family. No friends. Nothing. Just you. I want you to take this part very seriously. For real, what would you do? Would you hire a private chef? A private coach so that you can physically become that version that you want to be? Are you going to shamanic retreats? Would you learn something about gardening or yoga? How would you take care of *you?*

I think you'll see after you've done this that the super-responsible you may end up financially ahead, but at the end of a year, is she happier than she was before she came into money? Our conditioning has told us that this is the safest place to be, but is it fulfilling in any way? Number two might think she's happier than she was before, but in five, ten, and even twenty years, where will she be when the money's gone and she has to revert back to the lifestyle she had before the money? Will she have any friends left? The third column is where personal fulfillment and success come together.

By investing in yourself, realizing the importance of providing for your vision and your dreams, you are pushed to go further. It brings you to an edge of growth. It forces you to grow and to expand into a creative space where there is deeper knowing and understanding that you cannot access in the safe zone.

You cannot create an airplane when everybody tells you that humans can't fly. You may have heard the Reid Hoffman quote, "An entrepreneur is someone who will jump off a cliff and assemble an airplane on the way down." I would amend that to also include the self-actualized future millionaire and billionaire.

Success like this is impossible if you're not playing in that creative side of you that nobody but you has access to. If you're not watering the soil there, there's no way out of that. The best you can aspire to is that safe zone. The box you already know. And as much as external security might seem to fulfill you by promising to grow you $1 million the traditional way, there is no personal satisfaction. The super-authentic you raises your standards to that next level of who you want to become.

You can't get from here to there until you make a move. I know it's scary to think about this in reality, but now is the time to take your first baby steps toward that big, hairy, ambitious goal of yours, which you know is out there. Having eight figures in your salary is not the same as having nine figures. And it's not the same as having ten figures. There are levels of wealth with which we need to align our ability to believe what we can achieve. So when you are at X salary or charging X rate, but you know deep down you are capable of charging five times that rate, it's time to start stepping out of your comfort zone. Ask for six times, seven times, even eight! You need to align with your goals and your worth step by step.

The only real limiting factor between you and those big, hairy, ambitious goals—your biggest enemy, your biggest roadblock—is you. Your beliefs and the time you take to invest in yourself. If you're not well trained or equipped to get there, how are you going to get there? If you don't believe you can, then you most certainly can't.

As my girl Oprah Winfrey said, "I had no idea that being my authentic self could make me as rich as I've become. If I had, I would have done it a lot earlier." You can make choices today to begin tearing down your roadblocks and rebuilding your beliefs beyond just equality.

CHAPTER 12

SHIFT BEYOND EQUALITY

*Money is only a tool. It will take you wherever you
wish, but it will not replace you as the driver.*
—AYN RAND

I hope by now you feel confident that you are and have always been enough, and you are beginning to normalize your *very* big dreams around money, knowing exactly what you want your normal life to look like in the future. When you shift your mind and start believing in your self-worth, things start happening. You start getting promotions or getting paid more from random sources. I really hope that you are beginning to see some positive changes as you have progressed through this book and that it's as exciting to you as it is for me to watch you blossom.

Before I go any further, though, I want to issue a very important warning: don't give in to fear!

I have seen so many women start to taste the success they have always dreamed of, just to get nervous and back away. Their conditioning takes over, and they think, *It's too good to last, so it won't. Something is going to go wrong.* This cynicism does nothing but harm.

It's like we're always waiting for the other shoe to drop, and so we can't trust that reality is reality. We don't think it's normal to have money. Instead, we go back to normalizing the struggle, the fear around money that you now know all too well isn't normal. And because it's what we were taught, it's safe. It's almost comforting, in a twisted way, to not be as wealthy as we imagine we'd like to be.

At the same time, remember that if we aim for equality, the best we will get is equality, but that might not be the best we can possibly achieve. If your dreams exceed what the world would have you believe is enough, then shouldn't your *enough* exceed what the world defines as equality for you?

Both of these mindsets—reverting to conditioning and aiming only for equality—can lead to self-sabotaging behaviors that I want to warn you to watch out for. Don't do either of them!

If you see your bank account growing, celebrate it! Embrace optimism, and recognize that this progress is real. Avoid hoarding it away out of fear that it will vanish. That's contrary to what I've been trying to teach you. Trust and normalize the idea that you are worthy of abundance and that money will continue to flow when you believe in your value and remain open to new opportunities.

All right, now that I've got that out of the way, I want to remind you that money doesn't equal self-worth. But it is often a concept the world uses to determine value. As crass as it sounds, there's nothing we can say or do to change that. Money is a symbol.

In other words, the truth about money is that it is a social measure of something. Just like meters, inches, feet, pounds, and kilograms are measures of distance and weight, money is a measure. That's all it is. You can't actually eat it when you go to a restaurant or use it as a home. Money's not going to be on the menu or in a display case. It's just a tool we use to obtain what we need and want in life.

But we see money as this catalyst to get us the things we want, which is why we just crave money like crazy. Did you ever wonder why we don't crave other measurements the same way? Like having a house that is twenty feet tall or a car that is fifteen feet long? When you think of it that way, it kind of seems arbitrary, doesn't it?

Whether we like it or not, society has created a system where money measures a person's worth, even though we all can agree that a life isn't actually worth money. At the risk of sounding redundant, I want to restate this again: money does not equal our value as a person, because we are all valuable merely by being alive. When you realize money is nothing more than just a measurement, you can dive much deeper into yourself to find out how much you're really worth.

Truth is, money is not a need, per se. Not like food, air, or water. If you were on a deserted island, money would do you no good. You could have this fantastic wad of bills, and you'd still be in big trouble. You can't eat it. If you tried to wear it, it would crumble. You can't make a shelter from it to keep you safe or warm.

Yet somehow we've crafted this illusion and have become obsessed with measuring up.

THE ILLUSION OF TIME

In the last chapter, I introduced the idea that we need to stop thinking in a linear way when it comes to our self-worth and potential. I want to explore that a little further, in terms of the way we can think about our ability to make progress toward our dreams. I noticed that many of us have been trained to think that goals have to happen in a logical progression. Likewise, obstacles should happen in the same logical way.

Think of it this way. When you landed your first job, you had certain expectations about how much you should be paid and what you should do with that money. Some of your beliefs probably revolved around your limited employability due to inexperience and your understanding of what a person your age was capable of.

When you moved into your early adult years, you probably expected certain obstacles based on your observations of people at the same stage of life. You never had enough money to do what you wanted. You weren't qualified enough to make more money yet. You needed more education. You had to figure out how to pay for college, a house, a car, insurance, all the things in the adult world, without being paid what an adult would. Your dreams would never have included millions or billions in the bank.

When we have very big thoughts around money, we tend to fall into this pattern that one thing has to follow the other. How dare you dream as a college student of something as grand as funding an animal sanctuary, building a wing of a hospital, or sailing around the world when there are bills to pay? You haven't paid your dues yet, so who are you to think you can be that wealthy?

What scientists and quantum physicists have realized is that time and space are truly governed by gravity and the speed at which you're traveling through space. For our purposes, just like money, time is not necessarily linear either. Things don't actually happen or have to happen in the sequence that we've been conditioned to think they happen. We can actually have way more control of the future that we create for ourselves than what you've been trained to think is true. Because if we perceive that the only way to get more money is to get more education, more tools, more experience, and a better job, then we're handcuffing ourselves to a narrative that doesn't necessarily serve us.

Instead, you can decide, "You know what? I can do this. I am making money," and just kind of go into a bit of a warp speed mindset.

Everybody else is going to say, "You're crazy. It doesn't actually work this way!" You should know by now not to listen to them.

At the start of this chapter, I mentioned the dangers of the "safe" mindset. This relates to our concept of time. Maybe for you, the normal is that you don't earn as much as you deserve. Maybe it's that you struggle for money and with your career. Maybe you're still stuck in a negative loop of conditioning from your childhood, and normal is that you are not worthy of success.

Do you see that in all these instances, "normal" is based on the past? This is mind blowing, because if quantum physics is correct, then the past doesn't exist, nor does the future. Quite literally, we are perpetually stuck in the present moment, experiencing it from different perspectives. You're creating a perceived reality in your mind, which can be a bit unsettling.

This is the best way I know to describe the concept of time and how it applies to our journey. Look at the top left corner of this page. Now look at the bottom right corner. Do you notice that both exist regardless of where you place your focus? The writing in the top left and the writing in the bottom right exist simultaneously and independently, yet they are connected by every word in between.

The curious thing is that your visual focus brings each corner to life. They may conceptually exist, but they aren't real until you grace them with your focus. Another curious thing is that you can only focus on one corner at a time.

Now, think about your lifespan drawn on a sheet of paper. The day you are born is at the top left corner, and the day you die is at the bottom right. Beneath this sheet of paper, there are infinite other sheets, like a thick book, each with a different version of the story that unfolds between your birth and death. Conceptually, all these pages exist, but none can become your reality until you grace them with your focus. Just like with the initial sheet-of-paper example, you can only focus on one page at a time.

At some point in life, you've likely had something fabulous happen, and you thought, *I've done really, really well lately. I got promoted twice over and have a lot more money than I expected. But this week, nothing's happening. I'm screwed. I'm totally screwed. This success is not my new normal. Everything so far was just a fluke.*

But here's the thing: the point of creation for any success that you've ever had was the present moment. You're never truly in the future. And you're never truly in the past. You're always in the now. The truth is that you don't have to worry about the future, because it's always going to be the present.

The fun thing about this whole idea is that because the future is infinite, it is full of infinite possibilities. You have a choice to live a life consumed by fear of the past and terrified of the future (thereby boycotting any future success), or you can be fully present in this moment. You can take command of your thoughts and realize that your only point of power is in the now. You don't have power from some point in the past, nor can you control from some point in the future.

We get so anxious and fixated on the future that we forget today. We get so obsessed with the past that we recreate memories that prevent us from being in the present. You're only alive right now. You can only create from this moment.

THE ILLUSION OF EGO

We have this concept of self, based on what we think we know about ourselves. The problem is that our eyes perceive such a limited version of ourselves relative to who we really are and who we can become. This is actually science. Visible light only makes up 0.0035 percent of the electromagnetic spectrum. Think of all the possibilities outside this tiny percentage of what we are actually able to see.

Because time is relative, in a way you already are all those things that you want to be. You just have to stop looking backward at who you were before, thinking that that past defines your current present and broader self. The past doesn't have to define you.

Neither does your ego, according to popular belief. Our ego is composed of our thoughts and beliefs, memories and experiences gained over time, and it shapes our perceptions, desires, and actions. Ego is assessing your life based on the false belief that "you are what you have or what you do."[13] However, the "illusion of the ego" refers to the notion that ego does not exist, but believing in the ego and letting it define your identity can get in the way of you knowing your true self.

In Buddhism, the self is said to both exist and not exist, a concept known as *anatta*. This concept suggests that there is no ego, or self, at the core of our existence. Instead, our experiences and actions arise from a combination of five ever-changing factors, or *skandhas*: body, sensation, perception, will, and consciousness. Although they are in a constant state of flux, these factors create the illusion of self. This is why, when seeking self-awareness, you can only become aware of your sensations or perceptions, but never your core self.[14]

Studies in fields like neuroscience, cognitive science, and social psychology also challenge the idea of a fixed and independent ego, finding that our self-perception is flexible and alterable, and it is influ-

---

13   Wayne W. Dyer, "The Ego Illusion," Dr. Wayne W. Dyer (blog), https://www.drwayne-dyer.com/blog/the-ego-illusion/.

14   Neel Burton, "Why Your Ego Is an Illusion: The Buddhist Take on the Self," Psychology Today (blog), modified May 6, 2024, https://www.psychologytoday.com/intl/blog/ataraxia/202405/why-your-ego-is-an-illusion.

enced and manipulated by factors such as social context, cultural norms, and even physical and emotional states.

Given this perspective of the ego, if you are looking to change your future in any way, shape, or form, you need to understand really clearly your definitions in the past.

If you thought you'd seen the last of that pen and journal, I hate to break it to you, but whip that sucker back out and turn to a fresh page. Write the words "Illusion of Money" at the top of a sheet of paper. Then read through these questions, and choose at least four to write down a response to:

- What is the biggest illusion of money that you've been conditioned to believe in?

- Why do you need it? Why do you want it?

- What is it measuring for you?

- Why have you chased money for so long?

- What are you supposed to look like when you receive all that money?

- How is money going to define the pinnacle of success for you?

- Why has money been the only item on the menu of "success" until now?

- When it comes down to money, where have you made decisions throughout your life and perhaps in your career that are driven by measuring up to money?

- How has succeeding financially been more important than pursuing what really energized you?

- When have you chased success and been left completely drained?

- What would money do for you if you suddenly had enough?

Now write the words "Illusion of Time" on the top of the next sheet of paper. Again, choose at least four of the following questions to journal down a response to:

- How does your past define you?

- How are you predetermining your future?

- How has your notion of time kept you in the "good enough" frame of mind?

- How has fear of the future held you back?

- How do you choose to use time, today, in this moment?

- Do you want to keep on looking to the past, judging yourself for things done or not done?

- Do you want to keep thinking about the future and how it might be worrisome?

- How does time get to function from now on for you?

- What does the present moment even mean? Does it mean to you that you get to create rather than define yourself by the past?

- How are you going to use time to stop passing the

buck to someone else, saying, "Oh, it was my upbring-
ing" or "It was my parents"?

- Do you think you are limited because of all the responsibilities consuming your time?

Once you've done this, write down any other thoughts
that came up for you as you were working through the
questions. Then I want you to go back through everything
you've just jotted down and look for patterns in these
entries. What do you notice?

When you look at your written thoughts, you should be able to see
that these are excuses. These are the reasons you are consciously or
unconsciously using to keep passing the buck. They are your justifica-
tions against taking responsibility for the fact that you can create and
choose in this present moment to do something completely different
from what has happened in the past. They are limiting you with regard
to what you can achieve. Did you know you can use time to stop
passing the buck to someone else?

You can choose to blame your boss or employer for your current
income, but if you've been with me thus far, you're probably starting
to realize that maybe, just maybe, you're giving them way too much
credit. My friend, this is your movie. You are the director, and as such,
you get to keep all the credit, both the good and the bad.

Have you ever heard that story of the mom who lifted the car
off her child even though she'd never worked out a day in the gym?
If she tried to repeat that with a barbell of the equivalent weight, she

would never be able to do that again. But yet, somehow, she was able to lift the car all by herself.

I promise that wasn't part of her definition of who she was. It just happened. In looking at your definitions of your illusions of money, time, and self, I want you to decide right now, in this present moment, from this vantage point, first and foremost, who are you?

I'm sure you can see where we're heading here. Turn to another page, and write "Illusion of Ego" at the top. Again, pick at least four questions here to write a response to, and then jot down anything else that comes to mind as you consider the full list (think about the patterns you sense emerge):

- How do you describe yourself to other people?
- What about that description is rooted in the past?
- What is based on the future?
- How much of your concept of yourself is centered on the present moment?
- Who do you choose to be?
- What does that extremely giving and kind version of yourself (that you're choosing to become) do in the present moment?
- How does she operate?
- Does she dress differently?
- Does she treat herself differently?

- Does she give herself a lot more credit for everything she's achieved in her past—more so than looking down at what she failed to accomplish?

- Where is your concept of "self" limiting your progression?

As I have done this exercise with women in my workshops, I am always touched by their responses. I thought maybe you'd appreciate knowing you're not alone, so I'm sharing a few of their thoughts here:

- "Money is the measurement of success by society. So if I don't have money, the world will tell me I'm unsuccessful. That's a lie. Only I get to decide if I'm successful or not."

- "I always felt that money means empowerment for me. Money is the power. That's how I used to feel. Now I'm thinking, *Wait a second. That is my illusion. Money actually never had the power. I am putting meaning to it. I'm giving all my energy to money. The power is actually in me.*"

- "I don't think about money a whole lot. I definitely worry about my future. If you ask my kids, we've moved more times than they can count. They never ask for presents. They just ask that we not move again. So I definitely struggle with stability and worry."

- "I worry that I'm going to somehow get to the end, and I'm going to look back and just have not really actually accomplished much."

- "I have so, so many opportunities and so many positive things, but I worry it won't last, so I don't enjoy it while I have it."

As you can see, everyone has a different view of themselves, and their relationship with money is different. But it can be comforting to know that others are on the same journey.

FIELDS OF ENERGY

This is where things start getting a little bit crazy. Are you ready? I've been saying in this chapter that you can choose what potential is held for you within the future. I want to explain why I keep saying that. You might laugh at this, but I confess that I love to binge on learning about space travel, physics, the unexplained universe, all those things—but only when they are based on tangible science.

There's a scientific theory that helps explain why this reality doesn't have to be the reality that you choose to define the next moment (at least in my mind). It is called wave particle duality.

This fundamental quantum mechanics theory essentially says that what you focus on grows in potential. In other words, if you give your attention and intention to something, you are contributing to its existence. This is coming from the same place as Einstein's description that in this world, absolutely every possible imaginable outcome already exists.

I want you to stop for a minute and absorb what that means for you. You are able to create anything in a thought, and it can become a reality based on your focused attention. If I'm focusing my attention here, this reality has more energetic magnetism toward me. Let's say I'm giving my attention and my energy toward the trees. The energy I'm emitting is being responded to by those trees. Then the energy those trees and I share becomes what is called the "ethereal field of energy."

Ever heard the phrase "where focus goes, energy flows"?

Remember the reticular activating system we talked about in the previous chapters? Let's say I see someone wearing a shirt with a certain logo on it. By giving that logo my attention, the part of our brain that sees logos is activated, and I'm going to start seeing that logo more and more often. Sometimes this is referred to in the psychology world as "the yellow car phenomenon." We bring forward to our awareness what was previously in our periphery.

The fact is, *you* get to decide if you are the pinnacle of success. If you choose right now, that can quite literally be the definition of how you choose to be present. You can choose to say, "I'm so freaking successful that I'm never going to look back and wonder if I was successful enough, because effective immediately, I'm deciding that I'm measuring up to all my dreams and ambitions, whatever that might mean."

When you start deliberately living from moment to moment, decisively believing in your success and worthiness, anxieties inevitably fall away.

When it comes down to wave particle duality, things start becoming more tangible when you focus on them. This means that this ethereal field of energy brings our thoughts into being. I know this is getting a little "out there," and it's okay if you feel a little confused. The whole point I want you to take away from this chapter is that when you focus your mind on something, the universe is a willing participant in helping you make that happen. Your positive focus attracts positive energy; your negative focus attracts more negative energy.

I want to leave you with the understanding that intention and potential are always available to you. You and I know that you have infinite potential opportunities. The way to get where you want to go is to decide to focus on positively nurturing your energy, your potential, and your intention. Anything you deliberately create and focus on in your mind will dictate how your reality unfolds. Your reality can be shaped by your ability to direct energy toward your potential and intention.

Throughout this journey, we have worked on letting go of the baggage that has held you back until now. That proverbial rucksack is no longer weighed down by heavy burdens; I bet you feel lighter and more worthy of pursuing your dreams of wealth and abundance. Remember, you are enough and inherently worthy of achieving your ideals.

Dreams are like seeds, and your energy is how you nourish those seeds. Of course, seeds become only what you feed them. If you feed your dream with energetic garbage such as worry, distrust, fear, anxiety, and anger, you poison it, and it will never grow. However, if you feed it hope, positivity, belief, and joy, it will sprout and grow.

Imagine your dreams as tiny seeds filled with immense potential. Kind of like those dandelions we talked about earlier. Your thoughts and energy are the sunlight, water, and nutrients these seeds need in order to thrive. When you focus on nurturing your dreams with positive energy, you create a fertile environment for them to flourish. On the contrary, if you allow negative emotions to dominate, you stifle their growth.

Every moment is an opportunity to choose what kind of energy you want to cultivate. By decisively embracing how life gets to play out for you, you align yourself with the flow of abundance and possibility. Trust in your ability to create the reality you desire. Believe in your dreams, nourish them with unwavering faith, and watch as they grow into the magnificent reality you envision.

Remember, the power to shape your future lies within you. With pure intention and positive focus, you can transform potential into reality and dreams into accomplishments. You are enough, and you are worthy of every success and happiness. As you move forward, lighter and more empowered, embrace the journey with confidence and joy. Your dreams of wealth and abundance are within reach, and you have everything you need to achieve them.

> With that, you have now reached the final journaling exercise I have for you. On a fresh page, take at least five minutes to journal about a conscious decision you can make over the next week to take one pure, energetic step toward stopping yourself from swamping your potential and intentions. It doesn't have to be anything big—as long as you are taking at least one tiny step that moves you in that direction.

Remember, money is the measurement of your worth by the world's standards, and you are of infinite worth. It could be something as simple as looking in the mirror every day and telling yourself you are worthy of a raise. Or a new job. Or a higher-paying consulting project. It could be journaling about your plans every morning. Or spending five minutes listing all the positive changes you are seeing every night.

And here's your final prompt:

> "Today begins a new chapter. As of today, I ..."

Whatever makes the most sense to you, start putting your energy toward that right now, and I'm betting you'll see results before you know it.

ARE YOU ENOUGH NOW?

Do the one thing you think you cannot do. Fail at it. Try again. Do
better the second time. The only people who never tumble are those
who never mount the high wire. This is your moment. Own it.
—OPRAH WINFREY

Well, my friends. You've done it. You have come this whole journey through the valleys and the shadows, and guess what—you're still here! I'm so impressed and amazed with anyone who can stick with it to the end.

My sincere hope as we close out this journey together is that you have experienced multiple aha moments. I hope you have come to realize that all the change you want to make begins by you realizing you've always been the creator of your reality. And the good news is that you've already got all the tools to achieve absolutely everything you need and want for the rest of your life.

Your net worth has never been about your family lineage, who you know, your résumé, your social media profile, or even your negotiating skills. It has always been about you awakening to the realization of the masterpiece that you already are, as I have been saying through this whole journey. It's a leap to move from believing you are limited, finite, and flawed to knowing you are eternal, infinite, and more than enough in every way imaginable.

So the question stands: Are you ready to make that big leap happen? Are you ready to take full credit for directing your movie? Are you ready to say yes to who you've always been?

The number one person keeping you from earning what you deserve isn't your boss. In my experience, most women don't land their dream opportunity because they're working with finite, obsolete, and paltry strategies—this is how you look for a job, this is how you advance in a role, this is how you talk about salary, this is how you ask for a raise. You can no longer confine yourself to those common, archaic methods of getting ahead. It starts with knowing who you are and remembering that you are of infinite worth and creative power. Then, you can start in that place of "knowing" and let that immeasurable worth dictate your path.

Big résumés don't land you the big job. It has very little to do with being the most qualified, having the best résumé, or even getting lucky. Your greatness cannot be conveyed through a piece of paper, even a fancy diploma. It gets noticed because you exude it.

If you haven't yet, today is the day to get really clear on what you want. Go back to the last writing prompt and actually go into real depth on what life gets to be like as of today. You know now that the direction of your thoughts and energy is fundamental. It doesn't matter how eager you are to climb Mount Everest. If you don't have a road map or the right gear, you're going to end up giving up before you even reach base camp.

Your journey is your own and nobody else's, but I'd like to leave you with one final thought. You do not have to go it alone. Now that you are well on your way to wholeness and happiness, I suggest making a point to surround yourself with the right people. This is not always our loved ones. I can tell you this from experience. For the first few years when I was running my coaching business, my husband kind of sucked at moral support. I felt like he was bringing me down, consistently draining my energy instead of backing me up and empowering me and encouraging me. I know he never meant to do this, but that's how I felt.

I was achieving remarkable results. I made significant amounts of money, had a wait-list of clients, garnered media attention from around the world, and was invited to teach at Ivy League institutions and work with companies like Google. However, I quickly realized that I needed to address the negative energy affecting me. I had to set a boundary and say, "You know what, honey? I love you dearly. But when it comes to my business, there's a boundary here, because you deplete me, and I need to be energized."

Sometimes even our closest people might not be able to help us get where we want to go until we help them see our vision. It's crucial to share your dreams with the important people in your life and invite them to be the support you truly need. Show them what you need.

To his credit, my husband listened to me and did exactly that. From then on, he did his best to step back and support me from the distance I needed so I didn't feel suffocated.

Life has taught me that women like us need to surround ourselves with others who see the light within each other.

Surrounding ourselves with the right people exponentially accelerates what we can accomplish. When you put the right people in the right mix with the right tools and you build the right momentum, it takes on a life of its own. You will feel like you're part of something greater than yourself, and that's exactly when the magic happens.

You can keep the momentum up because you're part of a broader movement that ultimately makes the world a better place.

The World Economic Forum has found that the gender wage gap isn't forecast to close for at least 136 years. That's an abysmal projection, but it doesn't have to become reality. And if it seems too far in the future for us to do anything about today, I would hope that at this point in the book you know that you are incredibly wrong. You now know that you get to opt out of being part of these statistics, and furthermore, I would argue that it is your responsibility to now leave a legacy of change for women coming up the pipeline to prove the World Economic Forum wrong. Because they don't know you—not the way that you know you. You and I both know our worth, and the more we empower ourselves to continuously live in that place of worthiness, the more the rest of the world will come to reflect it back to us!

A compounding effect happens when one empowered woman meets another one. They potentiate each other and inspire everyone in their wake. It's very similar to the compounding effect in economics. Imagine someone approached you and said, "I have $3 million in cash or a penny that doubles in value every day for a month. Which do you want?"

Well, think about it. Which one do you pick?

It's pretty tempting to immediately take the $3 million in cash, because what kind of idiot turns down money like that in favor of a single penny? But let's play it out and see if that is the wisest choice.

On day one, you could have $3 million or a penny. Day two, and you could have $3 million or two pennies. Bleak. Day three, you can have $3 million or four pennies. You can see where this is going.

Twenty days in, your penny is now $5,000, which is nice, but when you think about that compared to $3 million, it's still less appealing.

At twenty-nine days, you have either $3 million or $2.7 million. Getting closer. And there are still two days left.

We're in a thirty-one-day month, so on the second-to-last day, you have either $3 million or $5.3 million, which makes your choice easy. And then, to finish it off, on the last day of the month, that penny has now become exactly $10,737,418.24. All because you did the opposite of what most people would do. You took the penny.

When you start learning and practicing the principles in this book, you're investing in yourself in a way that compounds over time. You're effectively choosing the magic penny. I can't promise you'll become a multimillionaire just by reading this book, because as you might recall, I don't get to direct your movie. You are the one who gets to decide how the movie unfolds. What I can promise is that you're going to be a much better human being and that positive improvements will flow into your life.

It's not going to be an easy journey. You, of course, know this by now. You will doubt yourself at times. Others will doubt you at times as well. But if you keep your course and don't let any drunken sailors steer you wrong, you'll find those moments and people who make all of it worth it and who will remind you, when you can't remind yourself, of all that you are and more. Sometimes, that is all we have to hold on to.

Gravitate toward women like us. We are your tribe. There are more of us out there than you might think. We are the ones who see the light in each other and in ourselves. We believe in the magic of the present moment and know that we are truly worthy, capable, and more than enough to transform it into golden opportunities. Embrace the power of this connection, and let it nurture and uplift you. Together, we can achieve incredible things.

A few hours after our dog Skipper died, I was in one of those moments, bereft and needing anything to ground me. My daughter Maya and I went to sit outside by our firepit overlooking the beautiful fields. We both sat in quiet contemplation, lost in thoughts and memories of Skipper, looking into the horizon, trying to make the best of an unseasonably warm October day. I suddenly perked up ... I swore I could hear Skipper's unmistakable panting. Thinking it was just my imagination, some sort of self-imposed grief mechanism, I didn't say anything. But I couldn't help staring in the direction from which the panting clearly came from.

And just as I was homing in on the all-too-familiar breathing pattern, Maya stood up and walked over in the direction of the panting, peering over the fields, calling to see if our two other dogs were in the vicinity.

"Can you hear that too?" I asked.

"Yes, I hear Skipper's breathing," Maya said.

Now we were both staring in the direction of the unmistakable panting—hearing it loud and clear. It went on for about another minute, and then it disappeared.

There is nobody on this planet who'll ever be able to explain it away or convince us otherwise: it was Skipper. She had never left and was with us right there, in that moment.

Tough times will always come. But even amid the pain and hurt, when you feel lost, broken, and unworthy, look around for clues. They are there for us to find; they've never left us. They've always been there. Silver linings are everywhere, waiting to reassure us that we're still on track. That we've never been broken after all.

Godspeed, my friend. Until we meet again, may your light shine brightly enough to make your dreams come true. But more importantly, may it shine even brighter so that you light up the path for generations of women who will grow up watching you glow. May your journey be filled with purpose, your heart with joy, and your spirit with unwavering strength. Keep shining, and never forget the incredible power you hold within you.

ABOUT THE AUTHOR

OLIVIA JARAS is a multifaceted professional, celebrated as a career and salary negotiation expert, best-selling author, dedicated mother, and accomplished athlete. She has made a significant impact by empowering women to achieve pay equity and career advancement through her innovative resources and coaching platforms.

With expertise spanning various industries, Olivia helps women recognize their worth, articulate their value, and confidently negotiate for the compensation they deserve. Her work is a beacon of inspiration, advocating for closing the gender pay gap and promoting financial empowerment for women everywhere.

A proud graduate of the George Washington University and Tufts University, Olivia is also a former triathlete on Team USA. Her journey exemplifies transforming life's challenges into opportunities for growth and wealth. As a luminary in women's financial empowerment, she is passionate about helping women understand their self-worth, enhancing their industry reputations, and increasing their earning potential.

Olivia also specializes in helping organizations develop and implement effective human capital and compensation plans, providing guidance on communicating strategies, closing equity gaps, and solving complex issues to improve retention.

Olivia's contributions have been widely recognized. She has been a contributing writer for *Entrepreneur* magazine, was an official member of the Forbes Coaches Council, and was touted the "Résumé Guru" by CNN. Her work has been featured in *Forbes*, CNN, the BBC, Monster, Fast Company, Recruiter, MSNBC, Lifehack, Learnvest, the World Economic Forum, and more.

An award-winning, international best-selling author of *Know Your Worth, Get Your Worth: Salary Negotiation for Women,* Olivia is at the helm of a movement teaching women to master their careers and increase their earning potential. As the ultimate gender wage gap expert, negotiation expert, motivator, and persuasion coach, she is highly sought after as a leader in her field.

Olivia empowers individuals to get exactly what they want out of their lives and careers by using tools they already have within themselves. Her diverse career, combined with her roles as a mother and athlete, makes her a powerful advocate for women striving for success in all aspects of life.